Challenges

Total Teacher's Pack

A unique teaching package with teacher development workshops and photocopiable resources.

Contents

INTRODUCTION TO *CHALLENGES*

a Challenge

We first thought of the title of this book after speaking to the inspired (and inspiring) head teacher of a secondary school in a working class district outside Warsaw. He was talking to us about all the problems his school faced and, despite them, the many achievements of his students inside and outside the classroom. They took part in science olympiads, sporting events, choirs, youth orchestras, theatre groups, chess competitions and many other activities. This demonstrated the kind of enthusiasm and challenge we wanted to inspire in our own material.

Our definition of a 'challenge' is a task that, while not easy to accomplish, is worthwhile and rewarding. A challenge requires patience, hard work and the ability to overcome problems. Many challenges also involve working with other people as a team to achieve goals that would be impossible to reach as an individual.

For many years, in both society and education, there has been a tendency to focus on activities that give instant reward and success. However, more and more young people are taking part in challenging activities like popular marathons, expeditions, extreme sports and voluntary work. Even in the unlikely world of computer gaming, game designers have found that the most popular games are those that are the most difficult, hence the expression 'hard fun'. The conclusion must be that a challenge is often fun because it is not easy; people enjoy being stretched and challenged.

b Challenge in the classroom

Within the English language classroom there is one obvious challenge: learning a foreign language in a few hours a week within a school context. The challenge is there for students (and teachers) whether we like it or not. It may sometimes look insurmountable but it is not if we break it down into a series of smaller tasks or 'challenges'.

In *Challenges*, each module contains a series of grammar and skills activities and builds towards final speaking, writing and listening tasks in which students can use the language they have learnt. Because these tasks are *achievable*, they build students' confidence as well as laying the foundations for communicative competence. In parallel, there are learner development activities such as self-checks at the end of each module that encourage students to be aware of how well they are progressing towards the greater challenge of learning English.

The theme of 'challenge' is also present in such topics in *Challenges 1* as helping others, dealing with bullying, living with disability and fighting fires. In addition, the story focuses on how a group of teenage characters, at both a group and personal level, take part in challenges. In *Challenges 1*, the characters participate in the Duke of Edinburgh programme *www.dukeofed.org*; they have to take up a new hobby, do exercise, help others and go on a group expedition.

The characters in the team provide positive role models for teenage students because they are doing something worthwhile and overcoming personal and group problems to achieve their goals. The story provides a springboard for education in citizenship: making students aware of their rights and responsibilities; helping others and working for the community; being a good citizen.

THE STUDENTS' BOOK

Approach

Grammar

▶ The *Get Ready* module revises basic structures that students will probably have seen before (e.g. *to be*/pronouns/possessive adjectives). The *Challenges Placement Test* can be used to check students' structural knowledge.

▶ In *Challenges 1*, there is grammar in two main lessons in each module. At this level, students need to learn structures gradually and systematically.

▶ All grammar is presented in context. Students read articles, stories and dialogues. They then focus on structures in the text.

▶ First there is a focus on form. Then students work out, in a guided way, how to use the new structure.

▶ Practice moves from easier, more guided exercises on form to more challenging and freer speaking and writing tasks.

▶ The final activity (*Your Turn*) always gives students an opportunity to use the grammar to talk about their own lives.

▶ In the *Study Corner*, students check their grammar knowledge and are guided to remedial exercises to deal with problems.

Sentence Builders

▶ Sentence structure has often been neglected in ELT even though most language groups have quite different syntax from that in English (e.g. verb position in Slav languages; adjective position in Latin languages). L1 interference causes mistakes of word order and these are usually more serious than other mistakes, such as those with verb endings, because they affect understanding.

▶ *Sentence Builders* focus on potentially difficult sentence structure which is often related to the main grammar (e.g. present, past and future time clauses). They systematically build up knowledge of common sentence structure in English and help students to construct a repertoire of patterns in their minds.

▶ Target patterns appear in texts, are focused on explicitly in *Sentence Builders* and are then practised in guided exercises. *Sentence Builder* boxes then remain as a kind of pattern bank which can help students when revising.

Lexis

▶ *Key Word* boxes in **Challenges 1** cover basic lexical areas (e.g. jobs, animals, houses, parts of the body). The boxes are usually linked to the *Picture Dictionary* so that students can check the meaning of the words there. *Key Words* help students to understand both reading and listening texts and gives them essential vocabulary for writing and speaking tasks.

▶ *Word Builders* focus on key lexical features and help build up students' capacity to organise and learn English vocabulary. Lexical features include collocation (e.g. play the piano/ride a horse), multi-part verbs (e.g. **find out** how it works), compounds (science fiction) and delexicalised verbs (e.g. have a shower). These spots also focus on what is traditionally called 'wordbuilding': the adding of prefixes and suffixes (e.g. the suffixes driv*er*/pian*ist*).

▶ *Key Expressions* are related to key functional areas from A1 and A2 in the Common European Framework (e.g. asking for and giving directions). For a full breakdown of CEF descriptors covered see the website.

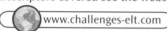 www.challenges-elt.com

There are other useful phrases in the story dialogues and these are focused on in the *Activity Book*.

Pronunciation

▶ Some pronunciation spots are related to the language presented in grammar presentations (e.g. questions / contractions).

▶ The main pronunciation spot is called *Listen Closely*. It focuses on problem sounds (e.g. /i:/ and /ɪ/) and on supra-segmental pronunciation work. One of the biggest problems students have with listening to natural English speech is actually hearing words and expressions as many words just seem to disappear. *Listen Closely* tasks focus on word stress, unstressed function words (e.g. *and* / *of*) and word boundaries.

Skills

▶ In **Challenges 1**, skills activities are guided, structured and, wherever possible, integrated with other skills. For example, in the *Get Ready* pages students listen to people speaking about a topic before they talk about the same thing themselves.

▶ There are **speaking** activities in every lesson and tasks always use language that has been presented to students (vocabulary, grammar and key expressions). Students are given time to think about their ideas and prepare for speaking as well as time to report back to the class what they have talked about in the pairwork stage.

▶ There are at least three **reading** texts per module. Text types include: magazine articles; interviews; questionnaires; brochures; non-fiction extracts; TV reviews; websites; notes, e-mails and postcards. There is also extra reading in the *Time Out* magazine at the end of the book: a story with three episodes; a poem; notices; quizzes; puzzles and guessing games.

▶ There are three or four **listening** tasks in every module. As well as the gist listening in the *Get Ready* section, there is a listening task in one of the main units. In the story unit, students read and listen to dialogues; this helps students see the relation between spoken language and its written form. In the *Across Cultures* sections, there is a listening text with both an extensive task and an intensive task. This task (*Listen Closely*) develops learners' ability to distinguish sounds, words and expressions. In addition, there are two songs in the *Time Out* section and one song in Module 9.

▶ There is **writing** in every module. In odd-numbered modules, there are projects which students can either do in pairs or on their own. Projects give students a chance to write about their own world and to be creative. Clear models and stages are provided to guide students. In even-numbered modules, Your Challenge spots focus on more interactive writing and students complete a form and write the following: text messages; different kinds of notes; a report; a postcard; e-mails. Students are also given clear models and the writing tasks are carefully staged.

Culture

▶ Cultural input appears throughout the book in both reading and listening texts.

▶ The story also provides cultural insights into the lives of the four characters who are doing the Duke of Edinburgh Bronze Award. The programme is run by a local youth club and the group go on expeditions to Devon as well as visiting the following places: an amusement park; the Bull Ring shopping centre in Birmingham; an animal centre.

▶ Finally, the *Across Culture* sections compare elements from different cultures rather than just presenting information about Britain. Students read about sport, festivals and schools around the world, find out about UNICEF and read about teenagers who have emigrated to Britain. At the end of the section, learners write projects about their own culture using the language of the reading texts.

Learner development

▶ One of the greatest challenges for students is to become better learners and to learn to study English on their own. Several features encourage learner independence in **Challenges 1**.

▶ On the *Get Ready* page, the objectives box clearly shows students what they are going to learn in the module.

▶ With each of the three main units, there is a corresponding spot in the *Time Out* magazine. This means that, when students finish early or have time to spare, they can look at the game, puzzle or quiz in the *Time Out* section.

▶ After students have done writing activities (*Your Challenge* and projects), they save their work for their own portfolio. Students build up their own portfolios as part of the Council of Europe Portfolio scheme. See p.38 for more information on the CEF.

▶ In the *Study Corner* students test what they have learnt in the Language Check and then listen and check their answers. In the *Feedback* section they can find out what areas they need to study more and are referred to the *Activity Book* for further practice.

▶ Finally, the *Study Help* systematically develops study skills. In **Challenges 1** there are spots about: classroom language; organising vocabulary books and learning words; using the *Picture Dictionary*; doing homework; organising grammar; working in groups; revising for exams.

1 Organisation

Challenges has a topic-based approach because it enables students to learn about the world through English and to learn the language at the same time. The course is divided into ten main modules plus a starter module. The starter module revises language that students have probably seen before, familiarises them with the course and develops their awareness as learners.

The themes in the main modules:

1. are related to **students' own world** (e.g. hobbies, music, television, amusement parks)
2. are **cross-curricular** (e.g. history, geography, science)
3. develop **citizenship education** (e.g. helping the community, dealing with disability)
4. are about other **cultures around the world** (e.g. sport, schools, festivals)

In *Challenges 1*, the ten main modules are organised like this:

1. a *Get Ready* page introduces students to the topic
2. two lessons have reading, listening, vocabulary and grammar
3. one lesson develops the story and has a major focus on speaking and writing
4. even-numbered modules have *Across Cultures* lessons with reading, listening, speaking and a project
5. at the end of every module there is a language check and learner development spot

At the end of the book there is a magazine section related to the units with fun activities like puzzles, games and reading for pleasure. Students can do the activities if they finish early in class or at home. There is also a picture dictionary that students can use to check new words in the units.

The lessons

▶ these boxes show teachers and students the objectives of each module

▶ these pages introduce the module topic

▶ lexical areas related to the module topic are presented

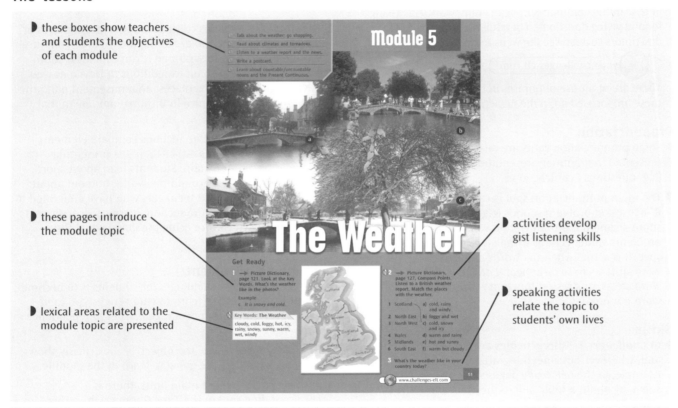

▶ activities develop gist listening skills

▶ speaking activities relate the topic to students' own lives

▶ these activities introduce the unit topic

▶ texts develop reading skills *and* present new grammar in context

▶ these spots focus on lexical features systematically

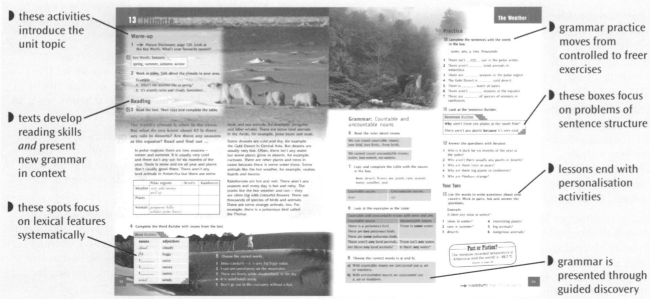

▶ grammar practice moves from controlled to freer exercises

▶ these boxes focus on problems of sentence structure

▶ lessons end with personalisation activities

▶ grammar is presented through guided discovery

▶ dialogues and photos develop the story

▶ functional language is focused on and practised

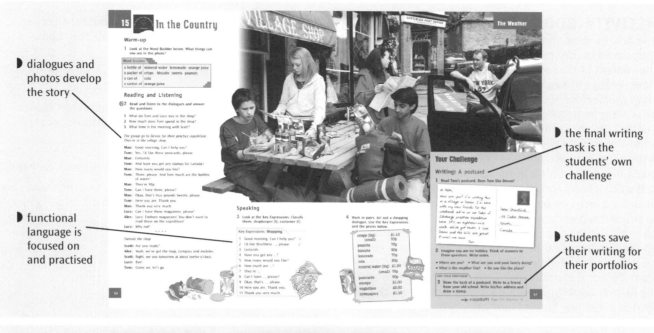

▶ the final writing task is the students' own challenge

▶ students save their writing for their portfolios

▶ texts look at culture around the world

▶ there is a systematic focus on basic prepositions of time, place and direction

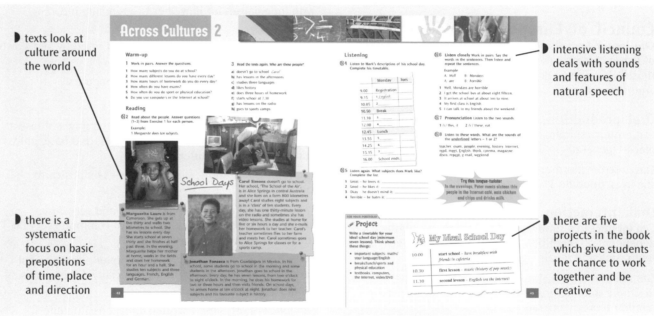

▶ intensive listening deals with sounds and features of natural speech

▶ there are five projects in the book which give students the chance to work together and be creative

▶ self-test exercises check students' vocabulary, grammar and functional language

▶ students listen and check their answers before doing extra revision

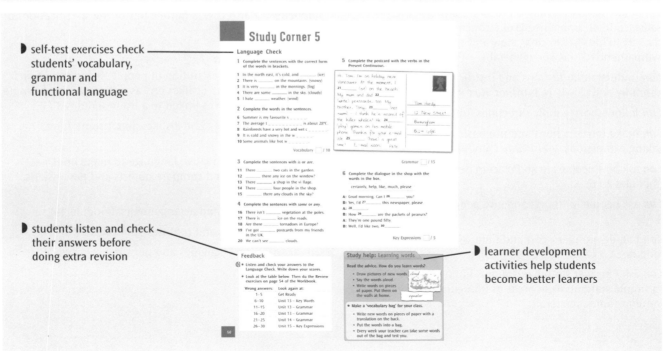

▶ learner development activities help students become better learners

ACTIVITY BOOK

The *Activity Book* gives further practice of the language introduced in the Student's Book. Each unit directly reflects the content of the corresponding unit of the Student's Book. Groups of *Key Words* and lexical features from *Word Builders* are recycled and practised throughout the book. Grammar structures and uses are practised in the Vocabulary and Grammar sections and exercises are graded according to difficulty with a one-, two- and three-star system. There is also a handy Grammar Reference section and a bilingual wordlist at the back of the book. Reading and writing skills are practised in the Skills unit, which also includes a focus on punctuation, they also practise key words and expressions. There are extra listening activities on every *Get Ready* page of these units. The recordings are on the **Challenges** CD-ROM. The *Language Check* in each module acts as a follow-up to the Language Quiz in the *Study Corner* of the Student's Book. Alternate modules of the *Activity Book* finish with a *Reading Corner*, which can be used as a 'reading for pleasure' activity or to give further reading comprehension practice.

Council of Europe

Challenges 1 covers all of the descriptors of the Council of Europe Framework at A1 level (Breakthrough) except those related to work and other adult contexts (e.g. making announcements):

Oral production A.1

Can produce simple, isolated phrases about people and places. (general)

Can describe him/herself, what he/she does and where he / she lives. (module 3)

Oral interaction A.1

Can interact in a simple way but communication dependent on repetition at a slower rate of speech, rephrasing and repair. (general)

Can ask and answer simple questions, initiate and respond to simple statements of immediate need or on very familiar topics. (general)

Can understand everyday expressions aimed at the satisfaction of simple needs of a concrete type, delivered directly to him/her in clear, slow and repeated speech by a sympathetic NS speaker. (general)

Can understand questions and instructions addressed carefully and slowly to him/her. (*Get Ready*)

Can follow short, simple directions. (module 4).

Can make introductions and use basic greeting and leave-taking expressions. (*Get Ready* / Module 10)

Can ask how people are and react to news. (modules 2 / 6)

Can ask people for things and give people things. (modules 4 / 8)

Can handle numbers, cost and time. (*Get Ready* / Module 5)

Can ask / answer simple questions, initiate and respond to simple statements in areas of immediate need or on familiar topics. (general)

Can ask and answer simple questions about themselves and other people, where they live, people they know, things they have. (module 2 / general)

Can indicate time – next week, last Friday, in November, three o'clock. (*Get Ready* / modules 6 / 10)

Can reply in interview to simple direct questions spoken very slowly and clearly about personal details. (general)

Writing A.1

Can write simple isolated phrases and sentences. (general)

Can write simple phrases and sentences about themselves and imaginary people, where they live and what they do. (general)

Can write a simple postcard. (module 5)

Can write numbers and dates, own name, nationality, address, age, date of birth. (module 1: completing a form)

Listening A.1

Can follow speech that is slow and carefully articulated, with long pauses for him / her to assimilate meaning. (general)

Can understand instructions addressed carefully and slowly to him / her. (*Get Ready*)

Can follow, short, simple directions. (module 4)

Reading A.1

Can understand very short, simple texts a single phrase at a time, picking up familiar names, words and basic phrases and rereading as required. (general)

Can understand short, simple messages on postcards. (module 5)

Can recognise familiar names, words and very basic phrases on simple notices in the most common everyday situations. (general)

Can get an idea of the content of simpler informational material and short descriptions especially if there is visual support. (general)

Can follow short, simple written directions. (module 4)

Challenges 1 also covers quite a few of the specifications of A.2 level:

Oral production A.2

Can give a simple description of people, living conditions, daily routines, likes / dislikes etc. as a short series of simple phrases and sentences linked to a list. (modules 3 / 4)

Can explain what he / she dislikes about something. (module 3)

Can use simple descriptive language to make brief statements about and compare objects and possessions. (module 8)

Can describe plans and arrangements. (module 10)

Can describe habits and routines. (modules 3 / 4)

Can describe past activities and personal experiences. (modules 6 / 7)

Oral interaction A.2

Can make and respond to invitations, suggestions. (modules 5 / 10)

Can say what he / she likes or dislikes. (module 3)

Can discuss what to do, where to go and make arrangements to meet. (module 10)

Can ask about things and make simple transactions in shops. (module 5)

Can give and receive information about quantities, numbers, prices etc. (module 5)

Can make simple purchases by stating what is wanted and asking the price. (module 5)

Can ask and answer questions about what they do in free time. (module 4)

Can ask for and give directions referring to a map or plan. (module 4)

Can say he / she didn't follow. (module 9)

Writing A.2

Can write simple, formulaic notes relating to matters in areas of immediate need. (modules 4 / 8 / 9 / 10)

Can write very simple personal letters / e-mails. (modules 6 / 7)

Listening A.2

Can understand and extract the essential information from short, recorded passages dealing with predictable everyday matters which are delivered slowly and clearly. (general)

Reading A.2

Can identify specific information in simpler written material he/she encounters such as letters brochures and short newspaper articles describing events. (general)

Can understand short, simple texts containing the highest frequency vocabulary, including a proportion of shared international vocabulary items. (general)

Can understand short, simple personal letters. (module 7)

Citizenship

Introduction

What is Citizenship?

At it's simplest, citizenship means being a member of a state or nation but it is used in different ways in different countries and contexts. Citizenship education can include a range of different concepts, including rights and responsibilities; helping others; actively contributing to the wellbeing of the school and the local community; learning about the institutions and practices of the society in which we live; and being a good 'global citizen', learning about our interrelationship with people and environments around the world and acting to make the world a better place.

Citizenship in *Challenges 1*

The activities suggested here focus on active local citizenship; contributing to family and friendship groups, school and local community; rights and responsibilities; increasing awareness of our interrelationship with the environment and other people. The young people participating in the Duke of Edinburgh Award, whose story runs throughout level 1 demonstrate 'citizenship' throughout, working as a team to encourage and support each other to learn new skills, take on new challenges and help in the local community.

How to use the Citizenship ideas

Activity ideas and key questions have been suggested which relate to themes in the text. Select activities that are most appropriate to your situation and to pupils' needs and interests. Discussions to develop ideas and understanding could be carried out in the pupils' first language but most activities contain outcomes that pupils should complete in English. Many of the activities involve collaborative group work, so that pupils have opportunities to develop and practise skills vital to Citizenship, e.g. listening, communication, empathy, negotiation, cooperation. The themes and activities can also be developed in other curriculum areas or in extra-curricular time.

Building lessons on Citizenship

MODULE 1: *The challenge*

Theme: Team work: What do I contribute to the communities I am part of?

Citizenship concepts: valuing diversity; interdependence; roles and responsibilities; cooperation

Purpose: To increase pupil's understanding that:

▶ everyone is unique, with different interests and abilities.

▶ everyone has a contribution they can make.

▶ everyone can develop new skills.

Class discussion

1) Ask students to share some of their interests from their pair work activity on page 15. Draw out the range of different interests and skills among class members.

   Do you use your interests and skills for the benefit or enjoyment of others, like Tom, Donna, Wei and Jimmy do on page 16?

2) Ask students to call out the different groups or 'communities' that they are part of (e.g. family, school, club, team, Internet chat room, local area). Write them on the board as they say them.

   Remind them that these communities work because the people in them have different roles and responsibilities and make different contributions.

   What contributions do you make to the different groups, for example, cook the dinner; design the internet site; cheer when they score a goal; make them laugh; play with them).

Individual activity: *For Your Portfolio*

List in English the groups you are part of.
For each one, complete the sentences:
This is what I do for my – : I …
This is what my – does for me: They …

Class discussion

Was it easy to think of what you contribute to and get from each group?

Were there any groups for which you couldn't think of anything you contribute?

What other contributions might you be able to make?

Would you need to develop new skills to do this?

MODULE 4: *Out and about*

Theme: Understanding the needs of others

Citizenship concepts: diversity; inclusion, accessibility, empathy

Purpose: To increase pupil's awareness of:

▶ the needs of people different from themselves.

▶ how activities and places can be adapted so that everyone can participate.

Class discussion

1) Ask students to share with the class some of the places they like to go in their spare time, which they will have talked about in the pair work activity on page 41.

2) Ask them to look at the pictures of the young disabled people on page 16.

Do you think Tom, Donna, Wei and Jimmy would enjoy going to some of the places you like to go to?

Are there any places it might be difficult for them to go to?

Are there any activities they might have difficulty joining in?

◗ How can they be helped to join in some of the activities?

Group activity

Tell students that their task, in groups of four, is to imagine that they had a visit from either Tom, Donna, Wei or Jimmy and to plan a day out with them in the local area, thinking about the following questions:

1 Where might they like to go?

2 How would you get there?

3 What would you do there?

4 How could you help them to join in the activities?

5 What else would you have to think about?

Individual activity: *For Your Portfolio*

Draw a cartoon strip of the day out with your visitor.

Draw:

the visitor arriving at your house, the journey to your chosen place, arriving at the place, joining in an activity

Add speech bubbles and labels in English.

MODULE 6: *Expeditions*
Theme: Welcoming strangers

Citizenship concepts: empathy, inclusion, helping others

Purpose: To increase pupil's awareness of and empathy with:

◗ how it feels to be a stranger.

◗ how newcomers can be helped to feel at home.

Class discussion

1) Remind students that all the stories in *Module 6* are about people going to places very different from those they were used to: the astronauts' mission to outer space; Marco Polo travelling across the desert to China; Alex, Lucy, Rajiv and Tom camping in the hills in thick fog; and Ada, Danil, Rodjin and Helen moving to a different country.

Ask them to say all the different words they can think of that describe how these people might have felt and write them on the board.

2) Has anyone in the class moved home, school, town or country? Or gone to a new club for the first time?

a How did they feel?

b What did they find difficult?

c What helped them to settle in?

Group activity

Tell pupils that their task, in groups of four, is to imagine that someone from a different town or country has either moved in next door to them, or has just started at their school.

◗ What might the newcomer find difficult?

◗ What could they do to welcome them and make them feel at home?

Class discussion

Ask the groups to share their ideas of how they could welcome a stranger and list the ideas on a board.

If the pupils were the newcomer, which response would they most like? Why?

Use the list to agree a school charter: 'Welcoming someone new to our school'.

Pupils could write the charter on large sheets of paper, or type it on the computer, to display around the school. They could introduce it at a school assembly.

Individual activity: *For Your Portfolio*

Imagine you had moved to a new town.

Write an e-mail to your friend, telling them how you feel on your first day in the new place.

MODULE 8: *Helping*
Theme: Improving our school environment

Citizenship concepts: environmental stewardship, informed action, taking responsibility

Purpose:

◗ To identify a problem in the school environment and work towards a solution

◗ To raise awareness that positive action must be based on accurate information

Class discussion

Remind pupils of the work they did on the themes of 'Helping' (page 77) and 'Change the World' (page 78).

What problems do they think there are in the school environment? List them on the board.

Tell the class that they are to choose one problem that they can research and do something to improve like Claire, Wayne and Adam did.

Discuss which problem they could easily do a survey about to find out more (e.g. litter, wasting energy, graffiti, biodiversity in the school grounds, cleanliness / tidiness, lack of facilities).

Group activity

Divide the class into small groups and allocate each group an area of the school buildings or grounds to survey.

Each group should make a sketch map of their area and mark on information that they think is relevant to the chosen topic, e.g.:

◗ energy: heat sources; doors or windows open when heating is on; lights or computers left on when not needed

◗ litter: location of litter; types of litter; location of bins; wind direction

Class discussion

Ask for feedback on the groups' findings:

- What was their most important finding?
- What were the main causes of the problem?
- Were some areas worse than others? Why?
- Would weather or time of day affect the results?
- What actions by people in the school made the problem worse?
- What actions by people in the school made things better?

Group activity

Ask each group to make a poster telling the rest of the school what they could do to improve things.

Where would they put their poster for maximum effect?

Individual activity: *For Your Portfolio*

Write a report in English about your findings:

The problem we researched was …

We did a survey of …

Our main findings were …

One solution would be …

MODULE 10: *Fun*

Theme: Planning a class celebration

Citizenship concepts: team work, roles and responsibilities, making a contribution, thinking of others

Purpose: For pupils:

- to use their skills to contribute to a group project.
- to think about the needs and interests of others.
- to reflect on their contribution.

Class discussion

Tell the class that they are going to practise their citizenship skills by working together to plan a class celebration or outing. Choose something that will really happen, e.g. a summer outing, a field trip, a religious or national festival or a class party.

Ask them to think of all the different tasks that would be involved in planning and carrying out the event (e.g. for a party or festival: food, decorations, music, activities, invitations; for a trip: transport, food, activities, letter to parents etc.) and list them on the board.

Ask them to volunteer to be part of a team responsible for one of the tasks.

Group activity

Each team is to work on the task that they have volunteered for. They must:

- research the task (e.g. what kinds of food, music or activities members of the class would like; who the class might like to invite (e.g. other pupils, staff, parents, school neighbours, local elderly people);

what kinds of transport are available and how much they cost, etc.).

- plan how to carry out their task including:
  - Who is going to do what?
  - By when?
  - What resources do they need? (money, materials, computer access etc.)
  - Who else do they need to talk to? (e.g. to get permission, information, help)
- Carry out the task.

1) Bring the class together at various stages of the planning process to see how everyone is getting on and to discuss any problems that may have arisen.

2) After the event

Ask the teams to reflect on the success of their activity:

- What went well?
- What could have gone better?
- What would they do differently next time?
- What have they learnt?
- What skills have they developed?

Can they think of other situations where this process would be used (e.g. in families, work situations, local or central government)?

Individual activity: *For Your Portfolio*

Write about what you have learnt from helping to organise this event:

- What did you do?
- What were you good at?
- What would you like to do better next time?

Glossary of Citizenship concepts

accessibility: the ease with which a place can be reached, entered or used – often used in relationship to equal rights for people with special needs, e.g. disabled or elderly people, those with young children

diversity: variety – used in the context of understanding and respecting differences between people

empathy: the ability to mentally identify with others – leading to sensitivity, interest in and concern for the needs and rights of others

environmental stewardship: taking responsibility for looking after the environment

inclusion: not excluding or 'leaving out' any individual or social group – making sure that everyone's needs are met

interdependence: dependence on each other – used to highlight that places and environments are inextricably interrelated and that individual and group actions (from shopping to political decisions) have an impact on other people and environments, locally and globally

Teacher development workshops

Introduction

Welcome to the Teacher Training section of the Teachers' Resource File.

In the Teacher Training section you will:

◗ Understand more about how teenagers learn

◗ Refresh your knowledge about how English works

◗ Understand more about how we teach English and how your students learn it

◗ Become more familiar with *Challenges 1*

◗ Complete tasks for the *teacher portfolio*

How each Unit is organised

You'll find that each Unit is organised in the same way.

◗ *Objectives*. These tell you what you are going to read about in the Unit. This is important as it gives you a clear focus for the Unit. Try looking back at the *objectives* when you have finished the Unit to see what you have done – and what you can remember. There are also *objectives* at the start of each *Module* in *Challenges 1* which tell the students what they are going to do. Have a look at *Challenges 1* page 33 for an example of the student objectives. You will find them at the top of the page, on the left. Try looking back at the *objectives* with the students at the end of each *Module* to remind them what they have learnt and what they have done.

◗ *First things first* and *Feedback*. *First things first* is the introduction to the Unit. There is always a short task to get you thinking about the topic of the Unit. Sometimes you'll have something to think about, sometimes you'll have something to do. All the *tasks* are short and practical. There is feedback on the task in the *Feedback* section.

◗ Then there are several short sections on the topic of the Unit. Have a look at *Teaching Reading* for an example. You'll see that after the *Feedback* section, there are eight short paragraphs. Each of these paragraphs has a heading, for example **Skimming and scanning** and each paragraph is written in clear, easy to understand language. After some of the paragraphs there are *tasks*. These *tasks* direct you to activities in *Challenges 1* so that you can see how the ideas work in practice in the course book.

◗ *Tips for the classroom*. This section gives you suggestions for things you can do with the students in the class. These are presented as bullet points and are always *practical* and *easy* to do.

◗ *Remember*. This section is in a box and includes four or five points. These are things it's really important to remember when teaching teenagers. They link the topic of the Unit to other Units in the book.

◗ *Over to you!* Each Unit ends with a section of ideas and suggestions for you to try out while you are teaching. You can compare ideas with other teachers too. The link to the *Challenges Website* will give you ideas of materials and activities to use in the class as well as up to date articles and website links.

Teaching Knowledge Test (TKT)

TKT is a new Cambridge ESOL test of teaching knowledge. The test is divided into three *Modules*. Each *Module* focuses on a different aspect of teaching knowledge. Find out more about the test by visiting: ***www.cambridgeesol.org/TKT***.

The Units of the ***Teacher Training Workshops*** in ***Challenges*** have been specially written to include concepts and terminology for TKT. So as you work through these Units you are preparing for TKT.

Teacher portfolio (TP)

You'll notice that in the *objectives* and in the *Over to you!* activities, there is mention of a *teacher portfolio*. This is your learning record or file. You may find it useful to keep a file of the notes you make when doing the *Teaching Training Workshop* Units. You can also make notes in your *teacher portfolio* of any new ideas and activities you try out in your classes from the *Over to you!* activities. It's also useful to write reflections of how successful the activities were with your classes and what you learnt from doing them. You can also make notes of your discussions with other teachers in your *teacher portfolio*. This will be a helpful collection of material, whether or not you intend to follow the TKT course.

Making the Units interactive

There are several *tasks* for you to do in each Unit. The *tasks* focus on *Challenges 1* and give you a chance to become more familiar with activities and materials in the course book. The *tasks* make the Units more interesting and the materials more interactive. This means that you are *doing* as well as *reading*. The suggestions in the *Over to you!* sections are also interactive because you'll try ideas out in class and write about them in your *teacher portfolio*.

Using the Teacher Training Workshop

There are different ways you can study the *Teacher Training Workshop* material:

On your own: You'll find that it's easy to study the units on your own. There isn't too much to read at one time, and the *tasks* make the material more interesting and interactive and help you get to know *Challenges 1*. *Over to you!* means you can continue to try out ideas after the Unit has finished too.

In a pair or group: You can study the material with other teachers. Try working through each Unit in pairs or groups and talking about the tasks as you do them. When working with other teachers you'll find that you learn lots of other ideas and you'll be able to find out what they do in their classes, too. You can also compare what you did in the *Over to you!* activities too.

On a course: You can study the material as part of a teacher training course. This means that you'll be part of a group and that the trainer will plan your work for you and work through the material with you, giving you ideas and feedback.

Teaching teenagers

In this Unit we will:

◗ Consider what is different about teaching teenagers

◗ Identify ways to help teenagers learn

◗ Become more familiar with the activities in *Challenges 1*

◗ Complete tasks for the *teacher portfolio*

First things first

Teaching teenagers is very different from teaching adults or young children. This is because they learn in different ways and are at a different stage of cognitive development. They are affected by social and emotional factors too. Look at the following chart. Tick what you think is relevant to teenagers.

Teenagers:	Yes	No
Show enthusiasm in the classroom		
Are shy in front of their friends		
Like working with members of the opposite sex		
Can analyse language		
Change from day to day		
Think their friends' opinions are very important		
Have a lot of background knowledge		
Don't have many different interests		
Are all at the same stage of development		

Feedback

Teenagers are very different one from another. This is because they are changing from being children to being adults, and because this change happens at different times and in different ways for different people. Very often teenagers are as confused as we are about their behaviour! If we understand why they are reacting the way that they are then we can help them be more efficient and effective learners.

Being cool!

Teenagers are becoming more aware of themselves in a group and of what other people think of them. For many teenagers, it's important to look *cool* and to be accepted in their peer group (their group of friends). It might not be *cool* for a student to answer all the teacher's questions for example, even if the student knows all the answers. The other students might think the student is trying to be too clever and that he / she wants to be different from the other students. So it's better to let students check answers or discuss their ideas in pairs or groups first before you ask for answers from the class. In this way students don't stand out or look different from their friends.

Being shy

Students who were enthusiastic and chatty in primary school can suddenly become very shy in secondary school. One reason is the change of environment. In primary school they were the oldest and they knew many of the people in the school. In secondary school they are the youngest and the school system and the people are all new. Teenagers' awareness of what others think of them can make some teenagers very shy. They are embarrassed to speak in front of their friends or to mime in front of the class. So it's better to do activities with teenagers which don't force them to perform or speak out in front of their friends. You will notice in *Challenges 1* that there are lots of activities where students work in groups but that there aren't activities where students speak out in front of the class, unless they choose to do so.

Growing up

Hormones also affect the physical development of teenagers. Some thirteen-year-olds look more like sixteen-year-olds. Other thirteen-year-olds look more like eleven-year-olds. These differences can make them very self-conscious. Hormones also affect teenagers' moods, how they feel. A teenager who is relaxed and friendly one day can be silent and unresponsive the next. It's important to remember that this behaviour is not usually in response to the teacher or the lesson but is because of what is happening inside their bodies.

Boys and girls

Girls usually mature earlier than boys. Thirteen-year-old girls will usually look older than thirteen-year-old boys. Teenage girls often have different interests from teenage boys too. At primary school, boys and girls often have the same interests, for example animals or hobbies. By the time they come to secondary school girls' interests are not always the same as boys' interests. You'll notice in *Challenges 1* that the topics of each *Module* are carefully balanced to appeal to both boys and girls, and that there are boys and girls as main characters in the story too.

Cognitive development

As well as developing physically and psychologically, teenagers are also developing how they think. We call this their cognitive development. Young children develop their thinking with reference to how they view the world around them and their place in it. For young children theirs is very much the world of concrete and real objects. For teenagers it is different. They are developing their ability to think in the abstract and to be able to think about their own thoughts. This is called their *metacognitive* ability. One of the aspects of metacognitive development is that teenagers can begin to analyse language: they can talk about grammar and language. One of the other aspects of metacognitive development is their ability to begin to reflect on their own learning and to identify what they are good at and what they need to work on. They can *self-assess*.

But teenagers don't all develop the same metacognitive skills and abilities at the same time. We can see the physical development but we can't see their metacognitive development. So we need to find out about this in different ways, for example by observing how well they can analyse language in classroom activities and how well they can *self-assess*.

The *Study Corners* in **Challenges 1** are designed to help students develop their metacognitive skills by gradually introducing analysis of language.

Interests and background knowledge

Teenagers have lots of interests and lots of background knowledge. But sometimes they are shy to contribute in the classroom so we need to encourage them by using group and pair work to give them confidence. Teenagers' interests may not be the same as ours. They will probably know information that we don't, for example the names of the newest rock bands or the most skilled footballers. Teenagers find it particularly motivating when they know something that their teacher doesn't and when we tell them so! One of the best ways of motivating teenagers is to *personalise* activities in the classroom. This means enabling students to talk about their interests and their knowledge and to use this knowledge to produce project work for other students to read. Many of the *portfolio activities* and *projects* in **Challenges 1** enable and encourage students to develop their own interests and contribute their own ideas.

▶ *For Your Portfolio* activity, page 29 of **Challenges 1**. Text messaging is very popular with teenagers. They can usually do it much faster than we can and they are much more familiar with the language of texting than we are. So this is an area where they can teach us something!

▶ *Project*, page 31 of **Challenges 1**. This project enables students to *personalise* the poster by making one about a sport that they are interested in.

Tips for the classroom

▶ Use pair and group work to enable students to check together before giving their answers or opinions in front of the class.

▶ Remember that silence does not mean that students aren't interested or that they can't answer.

▶ Plan how to pair and group students before the lesson. For example, decide if it's better to put students in same sex or mixed sex groups for different activities.

▶ Be aware which students find grammar analysis activities difficult and think of ways to help them, for example pair them with a student who finds these activities easier.

▶ Personalise activities whenever you can and encourage students to talk about their own interests and knowledge in classroom activities.

▶ Try not to single students out or over praise them in front of their friends.

▶ Don't take it personally! Remember that when students are silent or moody it's probably because of their hormones and their friendship groups. Try to avoid confrontations.

▶ Encourage students to talk about what they have learnt and how well they are learning.

▶ Teenagers respond well to positive feedback and praise.

▶ Don't label teenagers as 'bad' or 'lazy'. Think of why they might not be able to do an activity or react in the way you expect.

Remember ...

Teenagers do not all develop at the same rate.

Girls develop faster than boys.

Teenagers are enthusiastic and keen underneath.

Teenagers are easily demotivated.

Teenagers are very aware of what their classmates think of them.

Over to you!

Here are a few ideas and activities to help you develop your understanding of teaching teenagers.

Introduce a short session on a regular basis, for example ten minutes every two weeks, when individual students can talk about something they are interested in to the class. They can bring props, for example a picture, a photo, an object, and can talk for two or three minutes to the class. Don't force students to speak if they don't want to and have an activity of your own ready if no-one is ready to speak that day. Do the first talk yourself as an example.

Exchange ideas with other teachers, either face to face or using the Internet, on their strategies and techniques for teaching teenagers. Try out some of their ideas in your classes.

TP Try introducing pair work checks before eliciting feedback from the class, for example after a listening. Note in your *portfolio* if this technique seems to encourage students to speak more or not.

TP Look for and read more about metacognitive development in teenagers. Try out different ways of organising and managing your classes as a result. Make notes in your *portfolio* about what you did and why, and how successful it was.

www.challenges-elt.com

Working with beginners

In this Unit we will:

◗ Consider what is meant by beginner

◗ Identify how to work with beginners in the classroom

◗ Become more familiar with the activities in *Challenges 1*

◗ Complete tasks for the *teacher portfolio*

First things first

The word *beginners* is perhaps a little misleading. Our students are not beginners in everything. They come to the classroom with some knowledge and it's important to think what knowledge they are likely to bring with them and how that can help them learn. In your study group or on your own think of:

a) what world knowledge and experience your students bring to the class that will help them learn English

b) what knowledge of English they might bring with them to the classroom

Feedback

Teenage students will bring experience of learning in a school environment and will be able to apply many of the techniques and strategies they have used for other subjects to the learning of English.

Are there any real beginners?

It is probable that all your students will have some understanding of English. They may have met English in situations such as:

their primary school, on holiday, on menus, on advertisements, on the Internet, in music lyrics, in films, on CD and DVD cases, on aeroplanes.

In these days of technology and the Internet it's very unusual for students to be what we call 'zero' beginners. Most students will have heard some English before. Many students may have not spoken English before, but this doesn't mean they can't understand what they hear or read.

Build on what the students know

Learning is a process of building from the known to the new. In the classroom we usually help students build on their previous or background knowledge by using *Warm-up* activities at the beginning of lessons.

*Task: Have a look at the Warm-up on page 4 of **Challenges 1**. This is the first Unit in the book. What background knowledge can the students bring to this activity? How will this help them do activity 2 on the same page?*

We can help students build on what they know by the topics that we use in the classroom. ***Challenges 1*** uses topics that students will be familiar with, but develops them in new ways. In this way students can make use of their background knowledge and use what they know to help them learn what is new.

*Task: Have a look at the rest of the introductory Unit Get Ready in **Challenges 1**. Each of the topics on pages 6–13 will be generally familiar to students. What do you think will be new for the students in each of these sections and how are the students helped to understand the new information?*

Using English from day 1

It's particularly important for beginners that we, their teachers, use English in the classroom from day 1. We can use simple English for instructions and for giving feedback and praise. Of course we need to grade and select the language that we use, for example by using the imperative for instructions and by giving instructions in short sentences. But we shouldn't speak so slowly that we lose the natural rhythm of English. The more students hear us speak simple instructions (and we repeat the same ones every day!) the more they will understand them and get used to hearing English. We can help our students understand what we say by using simple gestures when we are speaking, for example by moving our hands from palms together to palms open when we say *Open your books*.

Giving students something to say

One of the frustrations of being a beginner used to be that students had lots of ideas but they couldn't say them. It took a long time for them to learn enough single words to build up useful and meaningful sentences and conversations. The way we teach beginners has changed and now students are given *key expressions* or *chunks of language* to learn, as well as words. Students can use these key expressions in different situations and it allows them to develop their conversational skills much more quickly.

*Task: Have a look at the Key Expressions in activity 5 on page 47 of **Challenges 1**. Now look at activity 6 and Your Challenge on the same page. How can the students use these expressions in each of these activities? How will this make them feel more confident and how will it help them extend their language?*

Thinking time

Beginners need time to think before they answer or give their ideas. You can develop different strategies for giving students more thinking time, for example tell students you're going to give them ten seconds' thinking time after you ask a question, let students check in pairs before asking for the answer, ask the question, give students the thinking time and then nominate a student to answer.

The balance of language and activity

Teaching beginners means that the language they are learning needs to be quite simple. We can't expect beginners to be able to use complex language. But we also have to make sure they don't get bored. We do this by giving them interesting and challenging activities to do. They can use simple language in activities which make them think and which they enjoy.

*Task: Have a look at activities 6 and 7 on page 19 of **Challenges 1**. The language, question words, is revision for the students from the last activity. How is the activity made challenging for the students? What knowledge do they need to answer the quiz in 7?*

Pair and group work
Pair and group work is very important for beginners. It gives them confidence and means they can share what they know. But students need to be trained to work in groups and pairs. They don't always do it naturally. Here are a few ideas:

▸ Make the first few pair and group activities quite short.

▸ Make sure students know exactly what they have to do.

▸ Give clear instructions about which students are working together. If you say *Get into pairs* there'll probably be chaos. Give students letters, for example A and B, around the class and tell As to work with Bs. Or point to students in twos and say *You two together*.

▸ Monitor the pairs as they are working. This means going around the class and checking that all the students are doing what you asked them to.

Once students are used to working in pairs and groups, you'll find that they quickly get into pairs and start working.

Frequent reviews and recycling
Beginners need frequent opportunities to review and recycle the language they are learning. This means that they need to reuse language from previous lessons on a regular basis. The structure and organisation of **Challenges 1** means that students get lots of language practice in new and varied contexts. There is also a more formal review of language in the *Study Corner* sections of each *Module*.

Using the mother tongue
There are times when it is necessary for beginners to use their mother tongue in class, though we should try to keep these uses to a minimum. On the other hand, we shouldn't view the occasional use of the mother tongue by students as an interference to their learning. One situation when beginners sometimes use the mother tongue is when we check instructions with them. We give the instructions in English and then we can ask them what they are going to do. They can reply in simple English, or they might reply in the mother tongue. Of course this is only useful if the students and the teacher share the same mother tongue! Some students might want to translate words or phrases into the mother tongue in their own mini dictionaries too. This use of the mother tongue is also useful for some learners. But it's best if the teacher avoids using the mother tongue in class.

Tips for the classroom
▸ Train your students how to work in groups and pairs.

▸ Use games for recycling and reviewing vocabulary.

▸ Make sure you use *Warm-up* activities at the beginning of every lesson.

▸ Build on the language that students already know.

▸ Build on the knowledge that students already have.

▸ Use simple, clear English.

▸ Allow occasional use of the mother tongue from students if and when appropriate.

▸ Encourage students to use *key expressions* they have learnt in other situations.

▸ Give students praise and encouragement.

> **Remember ...**
> There are very few 'zero' beginners.
> Students know more than they realise.
> Students may understand more than they can say or write.
> Practice makes prefect!
> Thinking time gives all students a chance to answer.

Over to you!
Here are a few ideas and activities to help you develop your understanding of teaching teenage beginners!

Audio record a lesson and listen to the tape. Make a note of all the times students use their mother tongue. Try and categorise which uses you feel are helpful and which not. Think of ways to help students use more English in the classroom.

Make a collection of words and phrases that students see around them all the time, for example on buses, on menus, etc. Display the words and phrases around the class and find out what your students can understand.

TP Introduce thinking time into your classes. Make notes in your *portfolio* as to how you think it works. Does it help students to answer? Ask the students how they feel about it.

TP As you introduce pair and group work to your class, notice how students respond to it and who works best with who. Make notes in your *portfolio* about different groupings and pairings for different activities and why you think these work.

www.challenges-elt.com

Classroom management

In this Unit we will:

▶ Consider the meaning of classroom management

▶ Identify how to improve our classroom management

▶ Become more familiar with activities in *Challenges 1*

▶ Complete tasks for the *teacher portfolio*

First things first

As teachers we are managers of our classes. But what does this mean? What kinds of things do we have to manage the class successfully? In your study group or on your own make a list of what you think classroom management includes.

Feedback

Compare your list with this one. How many of the areas are the same?

▶ The role(s) of the teacher

▶ The organisation of the classroom, for example seating, grouping, walls and environment

▶ Teacher language, for example giving and checking instructions

▶ Checking that everyone understands

▶ Getting everyone's attention

The role of the teacher

In the classroom teachers take on different roles at different stages of the lesson so that they can manage the class successfully. Examples of teacher roles are:

Planner	Planning the lesson
Monitor	Checking students when they are doing individual, pair and group work
Resource	Giving students help and advice

We take on different teacher roles at different stages of every lesson. The role we take on at each stage depends on the objective of that stage of the lesson and on the type of activity. For example, during the presentation stage of a lesson, the teacher is not only an informer, but also a guide for students to produce possible answers. During the practice stage, for example when students are doing pair work, the teacher is a monitor and a resource. During the feedback stage the teacher elicits answers and responses.

Think about the following things:

Task: What other teacher roles can you think of? Don't worry if you don't know the English names for them.

Task: Do students take on the same roles as the teacher? Do they take on different roles?

Students do not take on as many roles as the teacher does, and beginner students do not take on many roles at all. We need to support them in developing different roles so that, for example, they learn to manage and plan their work, to monitor each other in pair activities, to act as a resource for their classmates. Think about how you can do this in your lessons.

Classroom organisation

The organisation of the classroom can have a big effect on students' ability to learn. If students feel comfortable they will learn more easily, if students are in a stimulating environment they will be more interested to learn. Here are some of the ways we can organise the classroom:

▶ Change the layout of the desks when possible. Think about what layout will suit your lessons best (it's not possible to move desks for every lesson) and arrange the desks to suit you. Desks are often set up in rows, but this is not very good for pair and group work. Try organising the desks into work stations (blocks of four or six desks together) or a horseshoe (semi-circular rows of desks facing the teacher). Make sure you can easily walk around the classroom and talk to all the students.

▶ Change where students sit. Students like to sit in the same places in every lesson. It's a good idea to change the seating sometimes so that students are sitting next to new people and so that some students are not always at the back, or at the front, for example.

▶ Pre-plan how to divide students into pairs and groups for different activities. It's important to plan pairings and groupings before the lesson and regularly change who students work with. Sometimes this means students have to move to different parts of the classroom for pair or group work.

▶ Change the wall displays regularly. The environment of the classroom is very important. Students like to look around the room and notice what is on the walls. If we put students' work on the walls and change it regularly, they will be more interested. Posters also make good wall displays.

▶ Check the temperature of the room and the air flow. This sounds like common sense but it is very important for teenagers. Beginners get tired quickly and hot classrooms make them sleepy and inattentive. Don't forget to open windows to let in fresh air or to turn up the air conditioning. Cold classrooms are a problem too. So make sure it's not too hot or too cold and that there is always fresh air.

Classroom language

When working with beginners we have to think carefully about the classroom language that we use, for example to give instructions, to check they understand, to give feedback, to elicit their ideas and so on. We need to speak in English and the language needs to be simple and clear and the instruction needs to be short.

Task: Look at the following examples of teacher instructions. Tick (✔) the ones you can use with beginners and write a cross (✘) for the ones you can't.

1. *Open your books at page 12.*

2. *If you haven't already checked the answers on page 25, then do it quickly now and avoid talking about the possible answers until we have all finished.*

3. *Check with your partner.*

4. *Look at me.*

5. *Look at the piece of paper. Find someone in the class with the same colour. Sit next to them. Look at page 39 in your books and do activity 5. Write the answers on a piece of paper. Swap it with the group next to you. Check their answers.*

It is fine to use 1, 3 and 4 with beginners. They are clear, short and simple. But 2 and 5 are not appropriate for beginners. In 2 the language is too complicated and students won't understand. In 5 the language is simple but it is too long. There are too many instructions for students to remember. It's better to give these instructions in stages. For example, say the first three sentences first. When students are sitting together say the next two sentences. When they have finished the activity, say the last two sentences.

Task: Look at Challenges 1 page 63 Reading. Write out the instructions you would give to students for this activity.

Checking instructions are understood

There are always some students who don't listen when we give instructions so it's important to check instructions with students before they start. We can ask them *Do you understand?* But this doesn't tell us if they do understand or not. Students always answer yes! It's better to say, for example *Tell me what you are going to do.* This is also helpful for students who didn't understand your instructions, or who weren't listening the first time. They will have a chance to hear the instructions again.

Getting teenagers' attention

Teenagers are talkative and lively. Sometimes it can be difficult for the teacher to get everyone's attention. Trying to shout over their noise is not a good idea. You have to make more noise than them and very often the students don't hear you. It's much better to develop other ways of getting their attention. Here are some of the ways that other teachers use.

▶ The teacher switches the lights on and off or claps her hands.

▶ The teacher slowly counts down to one, for example three, two, one.

You will find that your students quickly learn what your technique is for getting attention and you will find that it is very effective.

→ See the Unit on Discipline for how to manage 'difficult students'.

In the classroom

▶ Plan how to organise the classroom. Try out different layouts for the desks and chairs. Get students to help you move the furniture.

▶ Decide where you want students to sit. Move them from time to time so they are not always sitting in the same places.

▶ Decide who you want students to work with. Plan this before the lesson.

▶ Use clear, simple English when giving instructions. Don't make instructions too long.

▶ Always check your instructions with the class by asking students to say them back to you. Don't ask *Do you understand?* or *Is that clear?*

▶ Choose a technique for getting students' attention. Make sure they are familiar with your technique and use it in every class.

▶ Appoint a few students to help you with the classroom displays. Change the students who help you every few weeks.

Remember, teenagers ...

need to be managed.

like routines and good management.

can help you organise your classroom.

can understand instructions in clear, simple English.

need fresh air and a classroom that's not too hot and not too cold.

Over to you!

Here are a few ideas and activities to help you develop your understanding of classroom management with teenagers:

If you find it difficult to give simple, clear classroom instructions in English try scripting a few and learning them by heart. Do you find this helps?

Think about other ways you could arrange the desks in your classroom. Is it possible to try them? Visit other teachers' classes. Do they have different desk arrangements? Talk to them about how these different arrangements work.

TP Reflect on the attention-getting technique that you are using. If it doesn't work, think about why not. Find out what techniques other teachers use and think about trying one of these.

TP Look back through your last lesson plan and think about your different teacher roles at the different stages. How did you act differently in the different roles? Did you use different language for example? Make notes in your *portfolio*.

www.challenges-elt.com

Discipline

In this Unit we will:

◗ Consider what discipline means

◗ Consider different discipline problems

◗ Identify strategies for maintaining discipline with students

◗ Complete tasks for the *teacher portfolio*

First things first

Teachers of teenagers often say that they are worried about discipline problems in their classes, for example that the teenagers don't always do what they say, that the teenagers use their mother tongue in speaking activities, that they are silent in speaking activities. On your own or in your study group, think of the classes you teach. What does the word discipline mean to you? What kinds of discipline problems do you have? How do you try and solve them?

Feedback

Discipline is the way a teacher keeps control in the classroom. We can build control strategies into our lesson planning and classroom management.

Discipline problems with teenagers

Teenagers are developing cognitively and are becoming more aware of themselves as individuals in the group. For some teenagers, this means being very quiet and not speaking out so that they don't look silly or stupid in front of their classmates. They might also feel it's 'cool' to seem uninterested or bored. For other teenagers, their growing self-awareness makes them want to show off in front of their classmates. These are the students who are noisy in class, who answer us back and can refuse to do the activities we set.

Discipline problems with beginners

A group of teenage beginners are a very mixed group. They will have different experiences of language learning (some will have learnt English before, some won't) and will be at different points of development (see the Unit on Teaching teenagers). This variety of levels and experiences contributes to discipline problems. Some more mature students in the class might feel a topic is babyish, other less mature students might feel that it is boring or too old for them. In both cases these students can cause discipline problems in the class. Another similar problem comes from the level of language of the students. Some students might find an activity is easy, finish it quickly and then start talking or messing around. Other students might find the same activity difficult and because they don't want to show that they can't do it, they also start messing around.

Some solutions

A discipline policy

It's important for us to know what the discipline policy of the school is and to make sure that we stick to this in our classes. It's a good idea to talk about the policy with the teenagers and to remind them what it is.

Rules

We must also have our own rules for behaviour in class. It's important that students know what this is from the first lesson and that we apply the rules fairly and firmly. Teenagers have a strong sense of fairness.

> **Task:** *Read through this set of rules. Which can you apply in your class and why? Which would not be appropriate?*
>
> 1. *Listen to other students when they are talking.*
>
> 2. *Listen to the teacher when she is speaking.*
>
> 3. *Use only English in the classroom.*
>
> 4. *Put your hand up when you want to speak / ask a question.*
>
> 5. *Put your hand up when you finish an activity.*
>
> *Notice that all the rules are positive (telling students what to do) and not negative (telling them what not to do). Why is this important?*

The best discipline policies are ones that the students and the teacher discuss, agree and monitor together. Here is an example from the list above. A student is talking about one of his ***Challenges 1*** *Projects*. Most of the students are listening, but three or four are not listening. They are messing about and talking to each other. One of the students who is listening puts up her hand and says *Some students are not listening. Can we start again?* The teacher then writes the names of the students who were not listening on the board and starts the activity again. The teacher does the same in other activities and then at the end of the lesson, the teacher collates the information about individual students and writes this in her notebook. Another method used by teachers is the 'football' method. The teacher has sets of yellow and red cards as used by referees in football games and issues them as warnings during the lesson to any students not keeping to the rules of the class. At the end of the lesson, students who have red cards are given some kind of punishment.

> **Task:** *In your study group or on your own make a list of rules for your classes. Think about how you can involve students in the process of creating and monitoring the rules, for example you can brainstorm ideas with the students, make a class contract and display the contract on the wall as a poster.*

Sanctions

All discipline policies need clear sanctions. This means that when students don't do what they are meant to do, something happens. Sanctions must always be realistic and enforceable. Whenever possible, sanctions should be opportunities for learning and not just punishments and where possible students should be given some responsibility, for example taking down the wall displays, helping the teacher carry her books to and from the teacher's room or cleaning the board. Students can respond well to sanctions which give them a role and a responsibility.

Task: In your study group or on your own make two lists, one of sanctions which are not realistic or which cannot be enforced, the other of realistic and enforceable sanctions.

Planning

It is important to think about discipline when we are planning our lessons.

Here are some questions to consider when planning lessons. Read through them and put a tick against the ones you think are most important:

Have I planned which students are going to work together in pair and group work?

Have I thought about when students will work in same ability pairings and groupings and when students will work in mixed ability pairings and groupings?

Have I planned where students will sit in the lesson?

Have I got some extra activities for early finishers?

Have I got a variety of activities in my lesson?

Have I thought about the instructions for all the activities?

Have I got all the materials ready for the lesson?

What lessons have the students had immediately before this one?

What time of day / day of the week is the lesson?

→ See the Unit on Lesson planning for more ideas on planning.

Task: Think about how each of these points can have an effect on discipline.

Getting to know the students

Teenagers are developing quickly and are very different one from another. By observing them in the class and making notes, we can build up a simple profile of each student. This is very helpful when we are planning pair and group work or giving responsibilities to different students, for example. We can also make notes of which students work well together and which work less well together.

A good teacher-student relationship with a class of teenagers is a delicate balance. It's important not to be too friendly. If we are, students will not respect us as teachers. It's better to be stricter than we want to be at the beginning of the year. Then we can become more relaxed with the students later if we want to,

but students know what our limits are and behave accordingly.

Praise good behaviour

Teenagers respond well to praise and to positive feedback. Praising students when they deserve it can have a very positive effect on discipline. It's easy to forget to give praise when it is deserved.

Tips for the classroom

▶ Set up a clear discipline policy with your students. Enforce it fairly and firmly.

▶ Involve your students in monitoring the discipline policy.

▶ Make sure your sanctions are ones you can enforce.

▶ Praise and reward good behaviour.

▶ Plan lessons carefully and develop your own personal planning checklist.

▶ Build up simple profiles of the students in your classes. Use these when planning. Update the profiles regularly and notice how your students change.

▶ Avoid stereotyping your students. There are no 'bad' students, only 'bad' behaviour.

> **Remember, teenagers ...**
> are trying to impress their classmates.
>
> have strong friendship groups.
>
> are of different levels of ability and have different interests.
>
> respond well to praise.
>
> enjoy being given responsibilities and involved in decision-making.

Over to you!

Here are a few ideas and activities to help you develop your understanding of discipline with teenagers;

Try out different techniques for managing discipline in your classrooms. Reflect on which seem most effective and why.

Discuss with other teachers what discipline problems they have in their classes and how they manage them. Share ideas and make suggestions. Meet on a regular basis to discuss how and whether discipline is improving.

TP Brainstorm and agree a set of class rules / a class contract with students. Agree on monitoring systems. Reflect in your *portfolio* on how well students keep to the agreed rules and how well the monitoring systems work.

TP If possible, arrange for a colleague to come and observe your class. Observe their class in turn. Discuss aspects of discipline in the two classes and compare ideas on how you both deal with these problems. Offer advice and ideas. Note the process and the outcomes in your *portfolio*.

www.challenges-elt.com

Mixed ability

In this Unit we will:

▶ Consider the meaning of mixed ability

▶ Identify ways of organising lessons and activities for mixed ability students

▶ Become more familiar with the activities in *Challenges 1*

▶ Complete tasks for the *teacher portfolio*

First things first

Many teachers talk about their classes being 'mixed ability'. In your study group or on your own think about what you understand by 'mixed ability'.

Feedback

Mixed ability means students studying in the same class whose level of language or ability is not the same. They are of mixed levels. This is in fact a description of every class of teenagers that we teach! Classes of teenager beginners will always be mixed ability. This is because:

▶ they are developing cognitively and some will develop their cognitive abilities faster than others.

▶ they are developing physically and some will develop faster than others and be more mature than their classmates.

▶ people learn languages in different ways. Some people like to think a lot before they speak, others are more confident about speaking out and don't mind making mistakes.

▶ some are more motivated than others to learn English. Motivated students usually make more successful learners.

▶ some are naturally better language learners than others.

▶ some will have learnt English before, others won't.

▶ girls develop faster than boys and often seem more mature than boys of the same age.

Not only is a class mixed ability, individual students have their own strengths and weaknesses: everyone has things they are good at and things they need more practice with. As teachers, we need to identify our students' strengths and think of ways we can give them more practice with the things they are not so good at.

Pairwork and groupings

It is important to plan ahead for pair and group activities and to decide before the lesson which students are going to work together. Sometimes it's better to have students working in same ability pairings or groupings. At other times it's much better to pair or group students who are of different abilities. In this way students can learn from and help each other.

*Task: Look through **Challenges 1** Module 4. Find one activity where you think students will work better in same ability pairs or groups and one activity where you think they will work better in different ability pairs or groups. Think about why this is.*

Controlling students' pace

In a mixed ability class, students finish activities at different times. Some will finish quickly, others will need more time. There are different ways we can manage this:

▶ Change the activity to make it simpler for some students and more challenging for others. This is called *differentiation*.

▶ Have additional activities ready for the students who finish early, the 'early finishers'. These should be activities which don't make them feel they are being punished for finishing first and which don't make the students who have not finished jealous!

▶ Remain flexible during the lesson and respond to the circumstances and the needs of the students.

*Task: Look at **Challenges 1** Project on page 67. How could you plan differentiation into this activity to make it simpler for some students and more challenging for others? (See possible answer below.) Would you have same or different ability groupings?*

Task: Which of the following additional activities could you give to students who finish activities early?

Word puzzles

Readers

*Activities from **Challenges 1** Time Out*

Help students who are still working

Extension Word Builder activities

You can give any of these activities to your students. It depends on the objective and stage of the lesson and how much of the lesson remains.

Some students take longer to do activities than other students. Sometimes the ones who finish quickly don't do very well. It can be helpful to ask the early finishers to check their work again themselves, to swap books with another student so they can check each other's work or maybe even to rewrite the activity. The ones who take more time often do better because they have taken the time to think and to reflect on what they are doing. It's equally important not to hurry students who haven't finished and to make sure that they are not made to feel stupid for taking longer to complete their work.

Teenagers' abilities

Teenagers are developing quickly and can change almost from week to week. A teenager who finds English difficult at the beginning of the year can be the star of the class by the end of the year. For this reason, it's a good idea to keep records of how students are working and of how they are developing. We also have to keep an 'open mind' about our students and not get fixed ideas about who are 'good' students and who are 'less good' students. Everyone has the potential to be a 'good' student.

Extra activities

When teaching mixed ability classes it's important to be flexible: to follow the lesson plan but to be ready to make changes to activities when necessary. For example, sometimes students take longer to finish an activity than we planned and we need to 'cut' something from the lesson. At other times students finish an activity more quickly than we planned and we need to add something extra to the lesson. The most useful extra or 'five minute' activities are ones where we don't need to prepare materials. In the **Challenges Class Handbook**, each lesson has suggested routes through the material and there are possible cuts if time is short, and things to do if there is extra time.

Task: Think of three or four 'five minute' activities that you could use with your classes. Remember the best ones don't need extra materials!

Remember mixed ability classes are the best ones to teach. They are the most interesting for the teacher and they are the classes where students can learn most from each other.

→ See the Unit on Dyslexia for how to plan to accommodate these students in your classes.

In the classroom

- Remember every student has their own strengths and weaknesses. Plan for your students' strengths and help them improve their weaknesses.
- Plan the student pairings and groupings for activities before the lesson.
- Vary student pairings and groupings.
- Plan for differentiation into longer activities.
- Make sure you have planned activities for early finishers. Keep materials and activities in a box in the classroom for these students. Encourage students to keep a record of the activities they have done.
- Make sure you always have one or two 'five minute' activities ready for every lesson.
- Keep regular notes on how students are developing so that you notice the changes and can change your planning and groupings to suit them.
- Think of your mixed ability classes in a positive way. Make the most of the mixed levels and abilities.

Remember, teenagers ...
are always mixed ability.

can learn a lot from each other.

develop and mature at different rates.

develop quickly and will develop new strengths.

are individuals and all have strengths and weaknesses.

Over to you!

Here are a few ideas and activities to help you develop your understanding of teaching mixed ability teenagers:

Try out self-grouping. Tell students what the activity is and then tell them to get into groups of three or four with whoever they think they will work best with. After the activity, ask the students how well they think their groups worked and why. Make a note of who is in which group and review how the self-grouping approach worked with your class. (It is not something to do every day but from time to time it is useful to see that students can be good at choosing the right partners.) You need to make sure that some students aren't left out.

TP Discuss with other teachers how they manage their mixed ability classes. Share ideas and activities. Try out some of their ideas and activities and make notes about this in your *portfolio*.

TP Plan for differentiation in the **Challenges 1 Project** sections. Keep detailed notes of this planning so you can vary the approach throughout the book.

TP Keep a note of how you pair and group students differently for different activities. Notice and record which groupings and pairings work best and think about why. Make a note of problems and / or talents that students have so that you can plan ahead.

www.challenges-elt.com

Answer to task

You could tell more linguistically able students that they have to write about their country in their own words and that they need to have five points about why they like their country and five about why they don't like it. The linguistically less able pupils could use the model as it is on page 67 and write three things they like about their country and two things they don't like.

Lesson planning

In this Unit we will:

▶ Consider the meaning of lesson planning

▶ Identify what to include in lesson plans

▶ Become more familiar with lesson planning in **Challenges 1**

▶ Complete tasks for the *teacher portfolio*

First things first

There are different things we need to think about when we are planning our lessons. In your study group or on your own, write down at least five things you consider when you are planning your lessons.

Feedback

Before planning a lesson, we need to know what the objectives of the lesson are. This means we need to know what the students are going to do in the lesson and what they need to learn or review to help them do this. You are using the same structure in this Workshop. Have a look at the top of this page for the four objectives for this Unit on Lesson Planning.

In **Challenges 1** the objectives are on the first page of each *Module*.

> **Task:** Look at **Challenges 1** page 23 for the objectives for Module 2. Notice that there is one objective for speaking, one for reading, one for writing, one for listening and one for grammar. Have a look at the first pages of the other Modules. Are there always five objectives? Is there always one for each language area?

Objectives say what the students are going to do with the language, for example Talk about … Read about … . This is important because it reminds us that language learning is about communication and outcomes.

Using the objectives

Teenage students are becoming more aware of their own learning. They are at a stage of development when they can think about what they are learning. At the beginning of each *Module* in **Challenges 1** it's helpful to talk to students about the objectives for the *Module* and then to talk about the objectives again at the end of each lesson and at the end of the *Module*.

See Units on Assessment and the Common European Framework for more discussion about how to work with the objectives.

> **Task:** Look at **Challenges 1** page 23 for the objectives for Module 2 again. Now have a look at the first lesson on pages 24 and 25. Which parts of the objectives will students do in this lesson?

Lesson stages

Successful lessons have different stages: they have a beginning, a middle and an end. Look again at **Challenges 1** pages 24 and 25. You will see that there are clear headings for different parts of the lesson:

Beginning: Warm-up

Middle: Reading, Grammar, Practice

End: Your Turn

These headings give you your lesson structure. The *Warm-up* is very important for helping students review vocabulary that they need for the lesson and for introducing them to the topic of the lesson. *Your Turn* at the end of the lesson is equally important. These end-of-lesson activities are sometimes called *Cool-downs*. They give the students a chance to review the language from the lesson in a relaxed and interesting way. In this lesson you will see it is a game.

Using the teacher's notes to help you plan

There are teacher's notes for every lesson in **Challenges 1**. These notes tell you how the activities work and give you the answers for the activities and the tapescripts. You can also use these teacher's notes to help you write your lesson plans.

Here is an example of how you might write an outline lesson plan for **Challenges 1** pages 24 and 25:

Class 6	Tuesday 5 November	10.15–11.15
Objectives: Read about sports stars Learn about *have got* and *'s* **Materials:** Pictures for *Warm-up* CD Teacher's Book		
Warm-up	About 5 minutes	Pairs then whole class
Reading (2)	About 10 minutes	Individuals then pairs then whole class
Reading (3)	About 5 minutes	Pairs then groups
Grammar (4)	About 10 minutes	Individuals then pairs then whole class
Practice (5)	About 5 minutes	Pairs then whole class
Practice (6)	About 2 minutes	Individuals then pairs then whole class
Practice (7)	About 10 minutes	Individuals then pairs then whole class
Practice (8 + 9)	About 10 minutes	Individual then groups then whole class
Your Turn (10)	About 5 minutes	Pairs then whole class
Notes and reflection on the lesson.		

Timing

It is important to decide before the lesson how long you think each activity will take and to try and keep to the timings when you are teaching the lesson. This gives the lesson a rhythm. If you don't decide on timings before the lesson, you might find that you spend too long on the reading, for example, and that you are not able to complete the Grammar sections or the pair work *Your Turn*.

Planning timing into the lesson also means you can plan for pace. Pace is the speed of the lesson. We vary the speed to keep students' attention. In this lesson, some activities are very short, others are longer. Some activities we do quickly, others we give students more time to complete. This also gives the lesson a rhythm.

Interaction

It is important to plan interaction into the lesson. Interaction is the way in which learners work together in class. We need to decide when students will work in pairs, when they will work in groups, when they will work on their own and when they will work as a whole class. This gives students variety. Pair and group work give students more chances to talk in English and also helps to build their confidence in using English. We also need to think about how we are going to pair and group students and decide who is going to work with who. It's boring for students to always work in the same pairs, for example.

Materials

Planning also means we have thought about the materials we need. For the lesson above the teacher is taking pictures for the *Warm-up*, the CD for the reading / listening and the Teacher's Book. When you teach four or five lessons in a day it's easy to forget something. So it's best to make a list of materials you need at the top of the lesson plan which you can check before going into the classroom.

Other things teachers often include in their plans are:

▶ Details about homework activities

▶ Detailed classroom instructions

▶ Answer keys. In *Challenges* these are included on pages of teacher's notes

▶ Names of students in different pairs or groups

▶ Ideas for extra activities, for example photocopiable activities from the *Challenges Resource File*

Task: *Make a list of other things you can include in lesson plans. Think of these things: anticipating problems, looking at background information, checking meaning.*

In the classroom

▶ Use the objectives in *Challenges 1* as a starting point for your lesson plans.

▶ Get into the habit of writing a short plan for each lesson you teach.

▶ Get into the habit of checking your lesson plan during the lesson. This is important for timing and interaction.

▶ Use colours in your lesson plan to make it easier to find your place during the lesson, for example highlight the pair activities in yellow.

▶ Keep your lesson plans as a record of what you have done with the students.

▶ Keep a note of different pairings and groupings on your lesson plans. After the lesson make a quick note of which pairings and groupings were successful.

▶ Write the objectives for the lesson on the board at the beginning of the lesson. Tell students that these are the objectives for the lesson and tell them what they are going to do in the lesson. At the end of the lesson read the objectives out again and remind them what they did in the lesson.

▶ Try sharing lesson planning with teachers who are teaching the same level and who are using the same materials.

Remember, teenagers ...

like to know what they are going to do in the lessons.

need variety in their lessons.

need changes of pace and interaction.

like working with different people.

can reflect on their own learning and learning objectives.

Over to you!

Here are a few ideas and activities to help you develop your understanding of lesson planning for teenagers:

Write your lesson plans for each class in a booklet. At the end of each lesson write brief notes on what was successful in the lesson and what was less successful. Get into the habit of looking back at your plans and your notes for each class on a regular basis.

TP Ask other teachers for examples of their lesson plans. Work in groups on designing effective and easy-to-use lesson plan frameworks. Try some of them out (use the framework and write your own plans) and make notes of whether you thought they were useful or not.

TP Try introducing new activities into your lessons (ones that are not in *Challenges 1*) and try changing the order of the activities in one of the lessons in *Challenges 1*. Make notes on what changes you made and why and if they were successful.

Look back at the objectives for this Unit. Did you do all these things? Do you have a sense of achievement?

www.challenges-elt.com

Assessment

In this Unit we will:

▸ Consider what assessment means

▸ Identify ways we can assess our students

▸ Become more familiar with the assessment in *Challenges 1*

▸ Complete tasks for the *teacher portfolio*

First things first

Assessment means finding out what our students know and what they can do. Testing is one way we can find out this information but there are some other ways we can find out what our students know and can do. Think about and write down how you were assessed when you were a student at school. Do you think assessment is different now? In your study group or on your own compare how you were assessed at school with what you think happens now.

Feedback

Here is a diagram to show different ways of assessing. Did you have these ideas in your discussion?

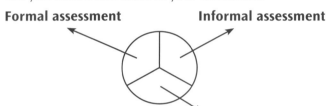

Formal assessment

Informal assessment

Self and peer assessment

Formal assessment

Formal assessment is tests and examinations. We don't give examinations to beginners, but we do give them tests from time to time. Students should know when they are being tested and tests should have a clear beginning and end. We can use tests to give us different kinds of information:

Placement Tests. We give *Placement Tests* at the beginning of the year. These help us to find out the levels of our students so that we know where to place them. You'll see that there is a *Placement Test* with **Challenges**. This will help you decide whether to start with Level 1 or Level 2.

Diagnostic Tests. We give *Diagnostic Tests* during the year. These help us find out our students' problems so that we can plan how to help them. We usually use the word *diagnose* to talk about doctors and their patients. If you think about this perhaps it will help you remember what the word means!

Progress Tests. This is the most common form of test we use in the classroom. These tests let us check each individual student's progress during the year. *Progress Tests* are usually quite short and contain the language which the students have just studied. For example in **Challenges 1** there are *Progress Tests* after each *Module*.

Achievement Tests. At the end of the year we can give students an *Achievement Test.* An *Achievement Test* contains a selection of the language the students have studied during the year.

Informal assessment

Informal assessment includes the different ways we gather information about what students can do in class, when they are working on everyday classroom tasks and activities. We informally assess student while they are working and often they don't know we are assessing them. There are different ways we can informally assess students:

Observation. We can watch students working in class and notice what they are doing well and what they need more practice with. It's useful to have a checklist of criteria, things we are looking for, and it's important to focus on only a few criteria and a few students in each lesson. We can't observe everyone in the same lesson! The *objectives* at the beginning of each *Module* in **Challenges 1** make a useful checklist.

Samples of work. We can collect pieces of work that the students do in class or at home. As with observation, it's a good idea to have a checklist of criteria and to collect work which we feel is a good example of one of the *Module objectives*.

> *Task: Have a look at the objectives on page 77 of* **Challenges 1***. Think about how you can assess these objectives both formally and informally. Look through the Module. What classroom activities could you use for informal assessment of these objectives? Are there any activities where you can collect samples of your students' work?*

Self and peer assessment

Self assessment is when students assess themselves. Peer assessment is when students assess each other. Teenagers are developing their ability to think about their thoughts and to reflect on their own performance and abilities, so both of these types of assessment are important for them. Self assessment helps teenagers become more aware of their own strengths and weaknesses and helps them become more independent. Peer assessment encourages collaboration and, as with self-assessment, helps students become more independent of the teacher.

> *Task: Have a look at Study Corner 1 on page 22 of* **Challenges 1***. Which of the following approaches to the material will help students become more aware of their own learning?*
>
> *a) Students complete the page individually. The teacher marks their work.*
>
> *b) Students complete the page individually. They check their own work using an answer key.*
>
> *c) Students complete the page individually. They check their work in pairs and discuss their answers. They check their partner's work using an answer key.*

See end of Unit for answer.

*Task: Have a look at the For Your Portfolio section on page 39 of **Challenges 1**. You'll notice that the students pass their reports on the class survey around the class and read them out. What types of assessment does this include? How will this help students to improve their work in the future?*

Assessing more than language

As language teachers, our main focus will be on assessing students' knowledge and use of English. But we also need to assess their non-linguistic skills and development, for example their attitude, their ability to work independently, their effort and commitment. These are often called *non-linguistic skills*. We can't test these non-linguistic skills, but we can assess them informally, through observation. Self and peer assessment are particularly useful in helping us learn how students are developing in these non-linguistic areas.

Marks and feedback

When we assess our students, there are two ways we can give them information about their progress. We can give them a mark or grade, for example B or 70% and we can give them written or oral feedback, for example *This is very good. Well done! Remember to check your spelling next time!* Feedback is personal because we comment on that student's work and progress. Feedback also gives students information about what they need to do to improve their work. A mark doesn't give them this information.

Assessing teenage beginners

When we assess teenage beginners, it's important to give them positive feedback about what they can do. Clearly beginners still have many things to learn, but we should stress to them what they can do. If we want our students to be motivated about learning, then we need to praise them and tell them what they can do well. Of course, it's important to tell them one or two things they need to improve each time so that they have a goal for their learning and so that they continue to feel motivated.

Tips for the classroom

▶ Make sure you assess your students informally as well as formally.

▶ Encourage students to assess their own work and progress (self-assessment) and to assess each other's work (peer assessment).

▶ Give students written or oral feedback as well as a mark.

▶ Give students regular feedback on their progress, making sure you start with a positive comment.

▶ Assess students non-linguistic skills as well as their linguistic skills.

▶ Use the *objectives* at the beginning of each *Module* in *Challenges 1* to help you plan your assessment.

▶ Let students check their tests together before you mark them with the class.

▶ Encourage students to collect samples of their best work in their portfolios.

▶ Use the results of tests and assessment when you are planning your lessons. These can give you valuable information about what you need to review and recycle.

Remember ...

assessment should motivate students not demotivate them.

assessment gives us information about each student's strengths and weaknesses.

to use different kinds of assessment.

to assess what you have taught.

peer and self-assessment are important for teenage students' development.

Over to you!

Here are a few ideas and activities to help you develop your understanding of assessment with teenagers.

Plan assessment checklists with other teachers for each *Module* of *Challenges 1* using the *objectives*. Try out different ways of assessing what your students can do and compare these with other teachers.

Make time at the end of each *Module* of *Challenges 1* to talk to students about their work and about what they feel they have learnt. Use the *objectives* and your assessment checklists to remind students what they *can do*.

TP Try out different ways of using the *Study Corner* sections in *Challenges 1*, for example using the ideas at the beginning of this unit. Note down in your *teacher portfolio* which ways seems to work best and why.

TP Give your students written or oral feedback for each piece of work that you mark, as well as tests that they do. Keep the feedback simple (the students need to understand it) and make sure you have a positive comment as well as a suggestion for how each student can improve. After two weeks, ask your students how they feel about the feedback. Make notes of their responses in your *teacher portfolio*.

www.challenges-elt.com

Answers to self and peer assessment task
b) and c)

Teaching grammar

In this Unit we will:

▶ Answer the question 'What is Grammar?'

▶ Consider different ways of teaching grammar to young teenagers

▶ Become more familiar with relevant sections of *Challenges*

▶ Complete tasks for the *teacher portfolio*

First things first

'Grammar' is everywhere. But what exactly is grammar? Either on your own or in your study group, complete these four sentences about grammar. There are many possible answers!

1. Grammar is ....

2. Grammar isn't ....

3. Grammar rules are ....

4. Grammar rules aren't ....

Feedback

Grammar can be difficult to define, so stating what it is as well as what it isn't can be a helpful way to begin. Grammar is the way a language allows us to combine words or parts of words into meaningful units. Units can be short, for example *a sunny day* or long, for example *We do projects at school every month*. Units can also be parts of words, for example *ed* to indicate a simple past tense in *washed,* or *es* to indicate the plural in *glasses*. Each of these units is a grammatical structure and each has a name, e.g. simple past, noun plurals.

*Task: Look through **Challenges 1** and find all the sections marked Grammar. How many different grammatical structures can you find?*

Grammar rules

Grammar rules help us to describe how a language works. But grammar rules can be a problem! They don't always work and there are many exceptions. There are several reasons for this.

▶ Language changes: something that was 'correct' twenty years ago is not 'correct' today.

▶ Most grammar rules describe written language and not spoken language and spoken language tends to change more quickly.

▶ There are different ways of describing grammar for beginners and for advanced students.

Grammar for beginners

When teaching beginners, we often have to make the grammar simpler. Have a look at **Challenges 1** Unit 13 page 52 exercise 6 for example. We teach beginners that *some* is used in positive statements and *any* in negatives and questions. We make it simpler to help

them understand. At higher levels we'll teach them that *some* can also be used in negative statements and questions. You will have heard: *Do you want some tea?* To teach beginners all these rules at the same time would be confusing. So we start with the basic rules and then, when we recycle a grammar point at a higher level, we often add another aspect of the rule.

Beginners can find language learning frustrating, especially when they want to express their opinions and ideas and can't do it in English because they haven't learnt the grammatical structure yet! We can help by teaching them *expressions* which they can use in different situations. These expressions or chunks might include complex grammatical structures, but students don't need to analyse them. They just learn to use them as they are.

*Task: Look through **Challenges 1** and find all the sections marked Key Expressions. Think about how these will help learners to express their ideas and opinions.*

Grammar for teenagers

Grammar is an abstract concept. Young teenagers are still developing their powers of abstract and analytical thinking, but this development does not happen at the same time for everyone. Some students develop this capacity earlier than their classmates. Therefore, the best way for young teenagers to understand how grammar works is to experience it in context first. In **Challenges Level 1** each grammar point appears in a text first: a story, a dialogue, a listening, a reading. The students focus on the meaning of the text before they focus on the key grammatical structures in the text. This makes the *grammar* section and the *practice* exercises more meaningful and memorable and means that students will be more able to do them.

*Task: Look at the text The New Fashion Models on page 24 of **Challenges 1**. Find all the examples of the grammar point have got / has got and the different ways it is used. When your learners read this text, do you think they will be more interested in the grammar or in reading about the models? Why is this important?*

Practice and mistakes

Learning grammatical structures is like learning anything new. The more practice we have the better we get. At first we will make mistakes. Mistakes are also important. They help us learn and we do better the next time. It's the same in the classroom for our students learning grammar. They need lots of praise when they communicate the message successfully (even if the grammar is not quite accurate) and they need lots of help and practice. We have to remember that mistakes are an important part of learning, and that we can help our students learn from the mistakes they make.

Task: Look through one or two Modules of **Challenges 1** and find the sections marked Study Corner. How do these sections give students the practice and the help they need?

Grammar patterns and models

Grammatical structures are not the same in every language, for example many languages don't have two present tenses, present simple and present continuous, like English does. Grammar rules will be different too, for example many other languages don't have the present perfect. So, it's important that we give students patterns or models to help them when they are creating their own sentences.

Task: Look through one or two Modules of **Challenges 1** and find all the sections marked Sentence Builder. How do these sections give students patterns and models to help them create their own sentences?

Grammar is important because it helps us communicate with other people. It makes what we say or write comprehensible. But we don't need to be 100% accurate to be comprehensible. Beginner students will make a lot of mistakes and we'll need to help them improve their level of grammatical accuracy. But we also need to praise them when they communicate successfully and respond to *what* they say as well as *how* they say it.

In the classroom

▶ Make sure students experience the grammar in context first before they do the practice exercises. Take time to talk to your students about the text and encourage them to use the grammatical structures orally before they do the written tasks.

▶ Get students to work and / or check the grammar exercises in pairs. It can be helpful to pair students with different levels of analytical thinking or language level. In this way one can help the other. Sometimes it's a good idea to pair students who are at a similar level too.

▶ Rather than asking your students to explain what a grammar point means, ask them to give you an example of the grammar point in a sentence. They will find this much easier and it will give you more useful information about how much they understand.

▶ Give your students lots of opportunities to review grammar in context in the lessons. Encourage them to talk about the texts, to ask questions and to express their ideas.

▶ Don't expect your students to use a grammatical structure correctly at the beginning. Remember *practice makes perfect*. Encourage them to use the language and give them positive feedback. Recycle as much as you can!

▶ Don't forget to tell your students when you understand the message of what they're saying or writing. They have communicated the message successfully – and that's very important.

▶ Don't assume that, because your students can use a grammatical structure, they also know its name and can analyse it. They may have studied English in primary school but the approach will have been different and the focus will have been more informal.

▶ Encourage students to use the *Key Expressions* from one lesson in other lessons, to help them develop their range of expression and confidence.

Remember, teenagers ...

are developing their ability to analyse grammar.

are at different levels of development.

need to experience grammar in context to understand the meaning.

may bring some knowledge of grammar from their primary classes.

may use grammar more confidently and accurately in spoken activities.

Over to you!

Here are a few ideas and activities to help you develop your understanding of teaching grammar to teenagers:

Look up one or two grammatical structures in different grammar books and compare how they explain the rules and which explanations you find clearer. Get used to checking grammar before your lessons using the grammar book you prefer.

Collect lists of student errors and prepare short exercises to give students extra practice in them.

TP Try out different ways of using the *Study Corner* sections of **Challenges 1**, for example students could do them in pairs and check with another pair after they have finished. Note down which ways are more successful and why you think that is.

TP Keep notes from your lessons on which grammatical structures students find easy or difficult to analyse. Try out different ways of helping them and reflect on which were more successful.

www.challenges-elt.com

Teaching vocabulary

In this Unit we will:

▶ Consider how we learn and remember vocabulary

▶ Identify ways of helping our students to develop their vocabulary

▶ Become more familiar with vocabulary activities in *Challenges 1*

▶ Complete tasks for the *teacher portfolio*

First things first

Vocabulary can be single words and groups of words. Learning a word or a group of words means learning many things about it. In your study group (or on your own) think about each of the following words and what students need to know about them in order to learn them:

paint, cool, slim, monitor

Feedback

Here are some of the things that students need to know:

Pronunciation	How we say the word
Part of speech	What kind of word it is, for example a noun or an adjective. We teach students the part of speech of the word in the context. We don't need to teach them, for example, that *paint* can be a verb and a noun.
Meaning	What the word means in the context. Words like *cool, monitor* can have different meanings depending on the context or situation. We teach students the meaning in the context of that lesson, not all its different meanings.
Spelling	How the word is spelt and other versions of the word, for example its plural.
Use and meanings	How and when the word is used. For example *cool* meaning *that's great* is used very informally. Negative or positive meanings. For example, if we describe someone as *slim* it has a positive meaning. *Thin* has a similar meaning to *slim*, but if we describe someone as *thin* it has a negative meaning.

Vocabulary in context

You will notice the word *context* appears in two of the explanations above. When we teach vocabulary, we always teach it in context. The context is the situation the word appears in in the lesson, for example the reading text, the listening text and so on. We need to teach the meaning of the word as it appears in

that context. It's sometimes possible for students to guess the meaning of new words from their context. You should encourage students to do this where possible as it is a very useful skill for students to develop. Students can also learn to deal with and learn new words on their own, either with the use of a dictionary or by guessing words from context.

New vocabulary

Everyone recognises and understands much more vocabulary than they use. We call the vocabulary students recognise and understand *receptive vocabulary*. We call the vocabulary students recognise, understand and use *active vocabulary*. You'll notice that in the *Challenges 1* reading and listening activities, there are quite a lot of words that students have not learnt. You'll find that they understand them from the context and some of these words will become part of their receptive vocabulary. You don't need to teach all the words in a listening or reading text to your students.

But it's important that students learn some new vocabulary in every lesson. Have a look in *Challenges 1* at the *Key Words* section on page 52. Students will not be able to understand the text if they don't understand the meaning of these words. They are also words that students use in the afterreading activity.

*Task: Look in **Challenges 1** at the Key Words sections. All these words need to become part of the students' active vocabulary. Are there Key Word sections before all the reading and listening activities? Why do you think this is? Will the Key Words become part of the students' active or receptive vocabulary?*

Presenting vocabulary

There are several steps students go through when they learn vocabulary. The first thing to remember is that students learn in different ways and so it's important to vary the ways we present or introduce the vocabulary.

Task: Look at the following list of ways of presenting vocabulary. Think of five different words and think of how you would present each one to the class using a different technique.

▶ *Using pictures, e.g. from the **Challenges 1** Picture Dictionary*

▶ *Using gestures (actions)*

▶ *Using translation*

▶ *Using the opposite or a similar English word*

▶ *Using the real object*

▶ *Using pronunciation*

Organising and recording vocabulary

Students need to record or write down the new vocabulary. It'll help students remember if they can link new words to words they already know. This will make it easier for them to remember the meanings of the new words later.

*Task: Have a look at **Challenges 1** page 22 and page 26.*

The example on page 22 is called a mind map and helps students to group similar words together. How many more Interests can you think of for this mind map?

The example on page 26 helps student organise words into different categories. The general topic is Food but, instead of creating a mind map, they divide the food words into different sets or categories. How many more foods can you think of for each category?

Recycling and reviewing vocabulary

We need to recycle or review vocabulary regularly to help students really learn the words. When we introduce new words in a lesson, students often seem to know them by the end of the lesson. But in the next lesson they have forgotten them! This is normal.

*Task: Look through **Challenges 1** at the Study Corner sections. These review the grammar and vocabulary from the Module. How many different ways is vocabulary reviewed in these sections?*

Students can also review words by checking them in a dictionary. Picture dictionaries are best for beginners, as the pictures help them remember the meaning of the new words.

*Task: Look at the **Challenges 1** Picture Dictionary pages 118–128. Notice that it is organised in meaning groups, for example Clothes, The Weather. Why do you think this is important for students? There are Study Corner activities, for example on page 32, to give students practice with using the picture dictionary. Can you think of two more short pair work activities you could do in the class to give students practice with using the Picture Dictionary?*

Vocabulary building

Students also need to learn how they can develop their vocabulary, for example how to make a noun from an adjective that they know. With beginner students we need to make these activities very simple. Look in **Challenges 1** at the *Word Builder* sections on pages 52 and 90. On page 52 students make nouns from weather adjectives that they know, on page 90 they make nouns from familiar verbs.

*Task: Look through **Challenges 1** at the other Word Builder sections. How is students' vocabulary developed in these sections?*

In the classroom

▶ Students learn in different ways so you need to use different ways of introducing vocabulary.

▶ Always teach new vocabulary in a context.

▶ Always make sure that you have checked the pronunciation of new words.

▶ Remember what students need to know to understand a word or phrase. Make sure you cover all these areas when you introduce new vocabulary.

▶ Remember to recycle and review vocabulary frequently. Games and short quizzes are a good way of doing this with teenagers for example from the **Challenges 1** Resource File or from the *Time Out* pages

▶ Make sure your students understand the *Key Words* before they do the listening or reading texts.

▶ Elicit other ideas for words from students for the **Challenges 1** Word Builder sections. Remind students of these sections when they are doing writing activities.

▶ Don't worry that students have not learnt the meaning of all the new vocabulary in a listening or reading text. They will still be able to understand it.

▶ Encourage students to use the *Picture Dictionary* when they are doing reading and writing activities.

▶ Use mind maps on the board to review vocabulary. Elicit other ideas from students on how they can review and record vocabulary.

Remember, teenagers ...

understand much more than they can say.

will need to be taught recording techniques such as mind maps.

get bored quickly, so words need varied presentation and review activities.

forget quickly, so need constant recycling.

can make connections between words in their own language and words in English.

can guess and predict meaning from the context.

Over to you!

Here are a few ideas and activities to help you develop your understanding of teaching Vocabulary to teenagers:

Before doing a listening or reading text with your students, choose about ten vocabulary items from the text that you think are important for them to know and which you want to become part of their active vocabulary. Check your pronunciation of the new words. Plan how to pre-teach this vocabulary. Pre-teach it and notice if and how students use it in the follow-up activities.

To help students review vocabulary, divide the class into groups of four and give each group a large piece of paper and a pen. Give each group a different topic, for example The Weather, Animals and tell them to make a mind map. Tell them not to look at **Challenges 1**. Display the mind maps on the walls and use them for review activities and games.

TP When people talk about vocabulary, they often use the term *false friends*. Find out what *false friends* means and note down any *false friends* you notice when you are teaching **Challenges 1**. How can you help your students remember and learn these?

www.challenges-elt.com

Teaching listening

In this Unit we will:

▶ Consider what listening involves

▶ Identify ways of making listening easier for students

▶ Become more familiar with how listening is managed in **Challenges 1**

▶ Complete tasks for the *teacher portfolio*

First things first

Students often say that they find listening more difficult than reading. We read written language but listen to spoken language. In your study group or on your own write down at least three differences between spoken and written language.

Feedback

Listening is one of the four language skills. Listening and reading are receptive skills and writing and speaking are productive skills. When we listen we receive and process input from spoken language.

Difficulties with listening

Spoken language is not like written language. Written language is fixed on the page. So when students read, they can read and reread the text and they can read at their own pace. Spoken language is different. Remember that when students listen:

▶ they cannot see the text on the page.

▶ they cannot control the speed that they listen.

▶ they cannot look back to an earlier part of the text.

▶ they cannot use punctuation to help them understand.

▶ they do not always know when one word finishes and another begins.

▶ they do not have pictures or text to help them make sense of what they hear.

▶ they may think they have to remember information to answer questions at the end.

It's easy to see why student often panic when they are listening. And when we panic we understand even less!

Beginners and listening

Students need to learn how to listen. When we teach beginners we do different kinds of listening. We give students tasks where they listen and read at the same time. This gives them confidence and helps them get used to hearing and understanding spoken English. This is important because words in English often sound very different to how they're written.

Task: Compare the written form and the sound of the following words: people, crossed, friend, listen, photo, season.

We also give students tasks where they listen to the CD without reading the text. When we do this, we need to make sure that the texts are short and simple and that the students know what they are listening for before they listen. This means that we set them a task before they listen. We often play the CD more than once so that students have the chance to listen again … and again … and again.

*Task: Look through **Challenges 1** and find an example of one Listen and Read activity and one Listening activity. How are they different?*

Reasons for listening

Listening is much easier if we know what the listening is going to be about, what the context is going to be. There are different activities we can do with students before they listen to introduce them to the context. We can write a word related to the listening, for example safety clothes for **Challenges 1** page 36, on the board and elicit their ideas, we can show them pictures and ask them to talk about them, we can teach them important words from the listening.

*Task: Look at **Challenges 1** page 36.*

Warm-up: How do you think this activity will make the listening easier for students?

Pictures: What can you ask your students about the pictures to help prepare them for the listening?

Read through the text in 2. Are there words that you will check your students understand before they listen? What are they? Remember they have to be important words!

Types of listening

There are different types of listening. Sometimes we listen to understand the general idea. This is called listening for gist. At other times we listen for specific information or for specific details. When we do this we listen more intensively. We need to give students a clear task before they listen so that they know what they have to do and what they are listening for. Normally the first task we give students is a listening for gist task. This introduces them to the general idea of the listening. After this we give them a task where they listen again for more specific information or details

*Task: Look at **Challenges 1** page 67 Listening. There are three tasks, 6, 7 and 8. Which task(s) is / are listening for gist and which for more specific information?*

Students always need to know what they are listening for before they listen. They need an activity or task to do, a chart to complete, boxes to tick and so on. We should never ask our students to listen without a task.

*Task: Look through **Challenges 1** and find at least four Listening sections. What are students going to listen for? What are the tasks?*

Successful listening

Listening to the CD from the book is not all the listening that students do in the classroom. They listen to you and they listen to each other. You are a very important source of listening for your students: you give them instructions, you elicit their feedback, you correct them, you praise them, you tell them to behave. And they can see you when you are speaking. Your gestures and your facial expressions all help them understand what you are saying.

Successful listening does not mean that students understand every word they hear. Successful listening is when students are able to complete the task or activity. Very often it doesn't matter that they haven't understood everything they heard. For example, if after listening activities students can discuss what they listened to and talk about how interesting it was. We should praise them for completing the listening tasks we set and remind them that they don't need to understand everything.

In the classroom

▶ Make sure you spend time setting the context for a listening. Use the pictures in the book, elicit ideas from the students, pre-teach or check important words from the listening.

▶ Make sure that students always know what their task is before they start listening. Always give students a task to complete while they are listening.

▶ Give students some thinking time after the listening and let them check their answers in pairs before you ask for answers from the class.

▶ Play the CD two or three times.

▶ Remember that you are an important source of listening for your students. Speak naturally and clearly.

▶ Remember too that students' classmates are also an important source of listening. Make sure they listen to each other, especially when a student is speaking in front of the class. Give them opportunities to listen to each other in pair and group work too.

▶ <u>Never</u> play the CD without setting a task.

▶ Only ask students questions after a listening task if you have set the questions <u>before</u> they listen.

▶ Check for any particular difficulties such as an unusual accent or topic or the speed people are speaking before students listen. Adapt the listening tasks if necessary.

Remember ...

before listening, set the context so that students know what the listening is going to be about.

while listening, make sure the students have a clear task to do.

after listening, talk about the content and the context with the students. Play the CD again and give them another more specific listening task or a speaking or writing task.

Over to you!

Here are a few ideas and activities to help you develop your understanding of teaching listening to teenagers:

For the next **Challenges 1** *Reading and Listening* activity that you do, choose about four important words from the text and pre-teach them to the students.

TP Try out different ways of setting the context for the listenings in **Challenges 1**. For example, bring in some pictures, brainstorm ideas from students, ask students to predict what they are going to hear. Reflect on which ones were more successful. Ask students for their opinions too.

TP For the next **Challenges 1** *Listening* activity that you do, devise an after-listening discussion task and try it out with your students. Reflect on how successful it was.

www.challenges-elt.com

Teaching speaking

In this Unit we will:

▶ Consider what speaking involves

▶ Identify ways of giving our students opportunities to speak

▶ Become more familiar with the speaking activities in **Challenges 1**

▶ Complete tasks for the *teacher portfolio*

First things first

Young children talk all the time. Often we can't stop them talking in the classroom. Teenagers are the opposite. They are often silent and unwilling to speak in class and to answer our questions. In your study group or on your own consider why you think this is and what you can do in the classroom to encourage them to speak more. Think of these points: the maturity of the students, the students' level of English, their level of confidence, the mix of boys and girls in the class, the students' previous learning experience.

Feedback

Speaking is one of the four language skills. Speaking and writing are *productive* skills and listening and reading are *receptive* skills. When speaking students have to produce language, they have to speak out so that others can hear.

Problems of teaching teenagers

Teenagers are often shy and sometimes don't have much confidence. They also don't want to look silly and make mistakes in front of their friends. The best way for them to avoid this is to keep quiet!

Speaking involves a number of different processes. Students:

▶ have to understand the input, for example the question that we ask them. For beginners this means translating it in their heads into their mother tongue.

▶ need time to construct their answer. For beginners this also means translating it in their heads from their mother tongue into English.

▶ need time to think of the English words and phrases they can use.

▶ need time to rehearse their answer by saying it to themselves in their heads.

Tips and solutions

All this takes time! Very often we expect students to answer our questions immediately without giving them time. It's very important to give them thinking time before they answer. One way we can do this is to get them to discuss answers in pairs before we ask members of the class for the answer.

Beginners and speaking

At beginner level, students do not know very many words or structures and so can find it difficult to speak more than a few words. And they have to come up with ideas too which takes even more time. One way we can help them is to teach them complete expressions to use when they are speaking. Have a look at **Challenges 1** *Key Expressions* page 74 for an example. Students can learn these expressions as complete phrases. They don't have to analyse them.

*Task: Look through **Challenges 1** and find other examples of Key Expressions. Think of situations when your students can use them in the classroom.*

Spoken English vs written English

English is very different when it is spoken and when it is written. Look at **Challenges 1** *Speaking* on page 93. Say the dialogue out loud. Now think about how different the words and sentences sound from how they look on the page. The table shows you some differences.

Task: Talk about these differences with a partner.

Written language	Spoken language
Punctuation and capital letters show beginnings and ends of sentences and questions.	The movement of your voice (intonation) shows beginnings and ends of sentences and questions.
Words do not have accents to tell us which parts have more force or emphasis.	Some parts of words are spoken with more force than others, for example we say **foot**ball.
Each word is separate.	Words run together to make a stream of sound, for example How are you? sounds like one word.
Letters are always written in the same way. For example 'a' can only be written 'a' or 'A'.	Letters do not have the same sound in different words. For example 'a' has different sounds in the following words: thanks, okay, team, are.

*Task: Look through **Challenges 1** and find the Pronunciation sections. Think about how they help students to get used to the way English is spoken.*

Helping students with pronunciation

We all agree that English sounds very different from the way it looks on the page. For this reason we sometimes teach students how to say words and expressions before they read them. When you pre-teach words for a listening or a reading text for example it's a good idea to:

▶ teach the meaning of the word or expression (see Vocabulary Unit for different ways you can do this).

▶ say the word or expression clearly for the students and / or listen to the CD.

▶ get the students to repeat the word or expression as a class and then in groups.

▶ write the word or expression on the board.

Reasons for speaking

The purpose of speaking is to communicate messages. We want to tell someone something, ask a question, answer a question and so on. It is the message which is important. In the classroom we often forget this and focus too much on the grammatical accuracy. We understand what a student is saying, but we correct the grammar rather than saying, for example *Yes, that's the right answer*. This makes beginner students nervous to speak because they are not sure their grammar is correct. We need to remember to focus on what the student is saying and respond to this as well as how they are saying it. We also have to remind students to listen to each other. Teenagers are sometimes impatient and don't listen to their classmates when they are speaking.

Different speaking activities

There are many different kinds of speaking activities that your students can do in the classroom. Some are more controlled, which means students do not have to create very much language of their own. Some are less controlled, which means students are freer to say what they want.

Task: Which type of activities do you think are better for beginners, more controlled speaking activities or less controlled speaking activities?

In *Challenges 1* there are many different controlled speaking activities. For example have a look at the *Speaking* sections on pages 21, 31, 47, 64, 93. Beginners need a clear framework for speaking activities and you will see that all these activities are very structured. The students practise the phrases they are going to use first before they do the activity in pairs and they use the same phrases, changing one or two words, in the pair activity.

Monitoring speaking activities

When your students are doing speaking activities in pairs, it's important to go around the class and listen to them working. This is called *monitoring*. You can encourage and praise them and give them help if they are not sure what they have to do. But it's best not to correct their language too much. If you do, they will probably stop speaking when you come near to them. Instead, you can make a few notes of the students' common problems. Then at the end of the activity you can practise this language again with the whole class.

Tips for the classroom

▶ When you ask questions of the students, remember to give them some thinking time before they answer.

▶ When it's possible, let students check what they want to say in pairs before they say it in front of the whole class.

▶ Don't over correct.

▶ Respond to the message, to what they are saying not how they are saying it.

▶ Praise your students when they speak.

▶ When students do the speaking activities from *Challenges 1*, monitor them and make notes of mistakes for a later activity.

▶ Encourage students to use *Key Expressions* in the lessons. Students can write their favourite *Key Expressions* on paper and display them. Remind students to use them when it's appropriate.

▶ From time to time, create quizzes and games which revise the *Challenges 1 Pronunciation* activities. Focus particularly on sounds your students have problems with. For example, choose pairs of words which have one sound the same, write each word on a piece of card, number the cards and put them around the walls of the room. Students work in pairs and match the cards.

▶ Remind students to use English in pair activities. Sometimes they will try and use their mother tongue.

▶ When you elicit answers from your students, ask them to speak out so all their classmates can hear. Don't repeat their answers yourself for the class! If you do, the students will learn not to speak out and not to listen to each other because they know that you will repeat everything.

> ## Remember, teenagers ...
> are shy and will be nervous of speaking out in front of their classmates.
>
> need a lot of practice in pairs before they feel confident to speak out.
>
> can often say more than you think they can.
>
> need thinking time.
>
> respond well to praise and encouragement.
>
> need time to think of ideas.

Over to you!

Here are a few ideas and activities to help you develop your understanding of teaching speaking to teenagers:

When students are doing pair activities, make a note of any expressions that they always say in their mother tongue. Teach them these expressions in English.

Try out different ways of encouraging your students to speak more loudly in front of their classmates. You might use a gesture or say *Sorry, I can't hear you* or ask a student at the other side of the class *Could you hear that?*

TP As you do *Challenges 1 Pronunciation* sections, make a note of which sections your students find more difficult. Make sure you review these sections in later lessons.

TP Tell your students you are going to introduce *thinking time*. For example, tell them that you will give them ten seconds' thinking time before they have to answer questions you ask the class. Keep notes in your *teacher portfolio* of how this works. Increase or reduce the time if necessary.

www.challenges-elt.com

Teaching reading

In this Unit we will:

▶ Consider what reading involves

▶ Identify ways of helping our students to be better readers

▶ Become more familiar with the reading in **Challenges 1**

▶ Complete tasks for the *teacher portfolio*

First things first

We read all the time, even when we do not realise we are doing it! In your study group or on your own write down all the things you have read in the last week! Use the mind map to give you some ideas.

Feedback

What extra ideas did you think of?

Reading is one of the four language skills. Reading and listening are *receptive* skills and writing and speaking are *productive* skills. When we read we receive and process input from written language. But we don't read everything in the same way.

Reading for different purposes

When we read we usually read for a purpose. We want to find out some information, we want to pass an exam, we want to check the price of something in the supermarket and so on. It's the purpose or reason for reading which makes us read in different ways.

Skimming and scanning

Sometimes we read quickly to find out the general idea of a text or to look for very specific information. Reading quickly to find out the general idea is called *skimming*. Reading quickly to find very specific information is called *scanning*. Imagine you have just bought a copy of your favourite magazine. You sit down with a cup of coffee and quickly skim through the magazine to find out what looks most interesting. Then you scan the titles and look for key words to give you the general idea of the articles.

Reading for detail

Sometimes we read more slowly for the details. Imagine in the example above that you have found an article that looks really interesting. You then read the article slowly and in detail. This is called *intensive reading*.

Task: Look at **Challenges 1** page 90 Exercises 2 and 4. For which exercise do the students scan the text to find very specific information and for which exercise do they read for detail?

Task: Look at **Challenges 1** page 78 Exercises 2 and 3. How do the names in Exercises 2 and 3 help the students know which part of the text to read? How do the True / False sentences in Exercise 3 give students a purpose for reading?

How texts work

Reading is not only about reading the words on the page. Look at **Challenges 1** page 107 Exercise 2. As well as reading the text to get information the students can get information about the text from the map, the flag, the title and the way the text is organised.

▶ The map and the flag give the students the context. They tell them that the quiz is about the UK.

▶ The title *The UK Quiz* tells them two things: that the text is a quiz and that it is about the UK.

▶ The way the text is organised, the layout, is helpful for the students too as quizzes probably look like this when they are written in their mother tongue.

This means that before they start reading the quiz, students will have a clear idea of the content and the purpose of the reading. This will make the reading much easier for them. Remind students to look at these clues. Elicit their predictions about the reading before they read.

Beginners and reading

In **Challenges 1** you will notice that there are many *Reading and Listening* activities, for example page 82. These are very important for beginners. They can listen to the CD at the same time as they read the text. This helps them read at a more natural speed and read whole words and chunks or blocks of text rather than sounding out words as letters. It also reminds them that words look and sound different, for example *tortoises* (page 82). Students do not have to read aloud as they listen, but some students might find it helpful to quietly mouth the words along with the CD.

Reading aloud

It is important to remember that reading aloud is not really a reading skill. It is more a speaking skill. It's possible to read aloud without understanding what we read! At beginner level it's not a good idea to ask teenage students to read aloud to their classmates.

Teenagers are often shy and do not want to be embarrassed in front of their friends and the other students might make fun of them. Most reading that our students do in class should be silent reading, or reading quietly along with the CD. There are a few times when students might read aloud in the classroom. They might:

▶ read aloud an example sentence or answer they have written.

▶ read aloud a line from the reading text which is the answer to a question.

▶ read aloud a line or two from an article which they have found interesting.

▶ read aloud a poem or message they have written.

Reading for pleasure

Don't forget that students should also be given opportunities to read for pleasure. There are different reading texts in *Challenges 1 Time Out* and there is something for all students to enjoy. You can also have a class library of simple readers or magazines for students to borrow and read at home. Make sure you talk to students about what they read. If you are interested in what they read they will want to read more and want to talk about it to you and to the class.

Extra practice

To give beginner students extra practice in reading, it's a good idea to put classroom language on pieces of paper around the walls. This reminds them of the language to use and also gives them practice in reading. Here is some useful language: *How do you spell … ? Can I borrow your … ? Can I go to the bathroom? What does … mean? Can you repeat that please?*

Tips for the classroom

▶ Make sure you spend time using the pictures and the layout to set the context of the reading before the students read. Encourage them to predict what they are going to read about.

▶ Pre-teach or check important words, using the pictures on the page, before students read the text.

▶ Give students time to read the tasks and check they understand what they have to do before they start reading.

▶ Set the first reading task before students start reading. This is usually a skimming or scanning task.

▶ Set a time limit for skimming and scanning tasks to encourage students to read quickly to find the information. Give students more time for more intensive reading tasks and activities.

▶ Encourage students to check their answers to tasks and activities in pairs before you check with the class.

▶ Encourage students to guess the meaning of words from the context. This is an important skill which should be encouraged.

▶ Encourage students to look back at the text when they are checking in their pairs.

▶ Don't ask students to read aloud unless there is a clear purpose and reason for them to do so.

▶ Write useful classroom language on pieces of paper and stick them around the walls. When students ask you for this in their mother tongue, or when they ask you in English and make a mistake, point at the paper on the wall. Students will quickly learn to look at the wall before they ask. Change the sentences and questions regularly.

Remember …

before reading, use the pictures and the layout in the book to set the context so that students know what the reading is going to be about.

while reading, make sure the students have a clear purpose and a task to do.

after reading, talk about the content and the context with the students. Let students read the text again and give them another more intensive reading task or a speaking or writing task.

Over to you!

Here are a few ideas and activities to help you develop your understanding of teaching reading to teenagers:

Ask your students what they like to read in their mother tongue. If you can, introduce similar materials in English into your class or ask students to bring materials into the classroom.

For the next *Challenges 1 Reading and Listening* activity that you do, set students a time limit to do the scanning task and let them do the task and read the text without playing the CD. Let students check in pairs and then play the CD for them to confirm their answers.

Work with other teachers and set up a class library. Put the materials in a box and place the box in each classroom once a week. Encourage students to borrow materials and to keep a record of what they have read.

TP When your students read sections of *Challenges 1 Time Out*, talk to them about what they have read and ask them what they like best and why. Make notes in your *teacher portfolio*.

www.challenges-elt.com

Teaching writing

In this Unit we will:

◗ Consider what writing involves

◗ Identify ways of helping our students to develop basic writing skills

◗ Become more familiar with the writing activities in **Challenges 1**

◗ Complete tasks for the *teacher portfolio*

First things first

There are many different kinds of writing, from notes to friends to formal reports. In your study group or on your own write down all the things you have written in the last week! Use the mind map to give you some ideas.

Feedback

What extra ideas did you think of?

Writing is one of the four language skills. Writing and speaking are *productive* skills and listening and reading are *receptive* skills. When writing students have to produce language, they have to produce language for others to read.

You can see that writing is many different things. Writing includes a short informal note to a friend as well as a formal report for the school. We call these different examples of writing *text types*.

*Task: Look through **Challenges 1** at the Writing sections. Note down all the different text types that students practise. You will notice that they are all useful text types for teenagers.*

How and what we write depends on the audience and the purpose for the writing. The audience is who we are writing for and the purpose is why we are writing. Think how differently we write a story for a school competition and a story for a five-year-old child. The basic story is the same perhaps, but the language we use will be very different.

Successful writing

Writing is a complex skill. There are many things involved in successful writing. Look at the following list. Tick all the things you think that students need to do to become successful writers:

Spell correctly

Write clearly

Punctuate correctly

Use accurate and appropriate grammar

Use accurate and appropriate vocabulary

Use an appropriate style (formal, neutral or informal)

Use an appropriate layout (how the writing is organised)

Construct sentences and paragraphs

Organise ideas clearly and logically

Express ideas clearly and logically

You probably ticked everything in the list! It's true that students need to learn and practise all these things to become successful writers. But they cannot learn them all at once. They learn them step by step. In **Challenges 1** the focus is very much on the basics: spelling, sentence and paragraph patterns, grammar and vocabulary.

*Task: Look through **Challenges 1** at the Sentence Builder sections. This section helps students with learning the patterns of sentences. How will it help them build up grammar patterns for their writing?*

English spelling is difficult! Many English teenagers have problems with English spelling so it's not a surprise that your students do as well. But there are spelling rules which students can learn to help them. Check in your Grammar Book for the basic spelling rules and teach these to your students.

Beginners and writing

Models and frameworks are very important for beginner students. They give them an example of the text type they need to use. Students can look at the model when they are writing their own text. Sometimes they only need to change one or two words when they write their text. At other times they will need to change more. But it's important that the framework is on the page to help them.

*Task: Have a look at **Challenges 1** page 39 for an example of a model. How will this help students when they write? How much will they have to change?*

Beginner students need simple but realistic writing tasks to do. Students need models for most of these tasks but not for all of them. There are no models for the grammar exercises, for example. This is because grammar exercises are not really writing tasks. But there are real writing tasks which beginner students can do without a model.

*Task: Have a look at **Challenges 1** page 21. To fill in the form students only need to write single words. But this is a realistic writing task and one that we often do in real life. Why do you think students don't need a model for this task?*

The most difficult part of writing can be to think of what to write. We can help students by giving them ideas of what they can write about. Some students may have their own ideas and can write about these. Other students may not be able to think of anything and so ideas are very useful. Remember what they need to do is write something. It is not so important what they write about.

*Task: Have a look at **Challenges 1** page 83. In section 1 students are given some ideas of what they can write about. How could you present these ideas in your class?*

Planning writing

It is very helpful for students to talk about their ideas together before they start writing. This gives them confidence and time to think of and note down words and expressions that will be useful.

*Task: Have a look at **Challenges 1** page 75. In section 3 students can talk about these questions before they write their ideas. How will this give students speaking practice as well as writing practice?*

Successful writers plan what they are going to write, write a first draft, check it, and rewrite it perhaps two or three times before it is finished. Beginner students do not have to do this very often, but it is a good idea to get them into the habit of writing notes first, writing a first draft, checking each other's drafts and then writing a final draft whenever possible.

*Task: Have a look at **Challenges 1** page 85 Project. Students have to produce leaflets for their portfolios. Plan this activity so that students, a) talk about their ideas together, b) make notes, c) write a first draft, d) check each other's drafts, e) write final drafts.*

Correcting students' writing

When we read and mark what our students write, we need to make sure we don't overcorrect the grammar and the vocabulary and forget about the message. The main aim of writing is to successfully communicate ideas or information. We should not expect beginner students to use grammar and vocabulary which is totally correct. We need to be realistic about what they can do and give them appropriate feedback. Here are some examples of teacher comments on student writing which is designed to motivate students.

> Well done. This is a great leaflet. It's colourful and interesting. Next time check your spelling more carefully!

> What an interesting story. I love the ending. Don't forget that we write stories in the past simple!

In the classroom

▶ Make sure that students make use of the models in their books when they are writing.

▶ Give talking time at the beginning of writing tasks for students to share and develop ideas.

▶ Remind students to look back at the **Challenges 1** *Sentence Builder* sections to help them with their writing.

▶ Remember grammar exercises are not writing.

▶ Make time for teaching writing in the classroom. Don't set the writing tasks as homework.

▶ When working on the **Challenges 1** *Portfolio Project* sections, encourage students to work together and to check each other's drafts.

▶ When students say 'I don't know what to write about', brainstorm some ideas with the whole class and write them on the board.

▶ Always prepare students for writing and give them the time they need to write.

▶ When designing your own writing tasks, don't forget to give students a model for their writing.

▶ Don't set open writing tasks, such as '*Write about your holidays*' with beginners.

▶ Don't overcorrect your students work. Try to always write a motivating comment about what they have written.

> **Remember, teenagers ...**
> are shy and often say they can't think what to write about.
>
> need ideas from you and their friends for their writing.
>
> are used to writing e-mails, text messages and on their computers and write more slowly with a pen or pencil.
>
> always want to finish quickly.
>
> need encouragement and positive feedback.

Over to you!

If possible, let your students do some of their writing on computers. Talk to them about the differences between writing on computers and writing with a pen or pencil (freehand).

Encourage your students to keep spelling books with notes of spelling rules and to use these when they are writing. You can make posters of spellings too to display on the walls when students are doing writing activities.

TP Try out different ways of giving students ideas for their writing. Make notes in your *portfolio* of the ones which are more successful. Can you think why this is?

TP Ask your students what kinds of writing they do. Find or write a model for one of these text types and use this in the classroom with your students to give them practice with this text type. Keep the material in your *portfolio* for use with another class.

www.challenges-elt.com

Common European Framework

In this Unit we will:

◗ Consider what the Common European Framework is

◗ Identify the connections between the Common European Framework and *Challenges 1*

Languages within the Common European Framework

The Common European Framework of Reference for Languages (also known as the CEF) is a system of describing different language levels and competences. The CEF is available in different languages and is used to describe levels of competence in different languages across Europe. This means that students studying different languages, for example Spanish and German, in different countries can share a common and agreed level of competence. The CEF helps teachers to plan their teaching and to match their students' progress and level to a Europe-wide system. The CEF is also important for assessment. Different international language examinations are linked to levels within the Framework. This means that students, teachers and employers can link examinations to specific level descriptions as provided in the Framework.

Levels within the CEF

Descriptions of different language levels are phrased in the form of *can do* statements. They state what students *can do* at each level. There are six levels: A1 is the lowest, C2 is the highest.

A1. Basic User. This is the lowest level which is described within the Framework. It is also described as *Breakthrough* Level.
A2. Basic User. This is also described as *Waystage* Level. Levels 1 and 2 of *Challenges 1* and *2* cover all the key objectives of this level.
B1. Independent User. This is also described as *Threshold* Level. Levels 3 and 4 of *Challenges 3* and *4* cover all the key objectives of this level.
B2. Independent User. This is also described as *Vantage* Level. Levels 3 and 4 of *Challenges 3* and *4* cover many of the objectives of this level.
C1. Proficient User. Learners at this level are also described as having *Effective Operational Proficiency*.
C2. Proficient Use. Learners at this level are also described as having *Mastery*.

Categories within the CEF

Level descriptions are divided into five main categories or areas: Listening, Writing, Reading, Spoken Interaction, Spoken Production. There are descriptions within the CEF of what students are expected to be able to do at each level in each of these five areas. You will notice that the *objectives* for each *Module* of *Challenges 1* also always include the four main skills, Listening, Speaking, Reading, Writing. At beginner level it's difficult to separate Spoken Interaction from Spoken Production so the word Speaking is used to cover both in *Challenges 1*.

Objectives within the CEF

The level descriptions within the CEF are also called *competences* or *objectives*. The *objectives* in *Challenges 1* are written in a similar way to the *objectives* in the CEF. Have a look at the objectives on page 77 of *Challenges 1*. You will notice that these *objectives* are all phrased as things students are going to do / can do.

Self-assessment within the CEF

The *objectives* for each skill at each level within the CEF are used to provide students with a checklist of *what they can do*. In this way students develop their ability to assess their own progress and development: self-assessment. Self-assessment is particularly important for teenage students who are developing their metacognitive skills, their ability to think about their own thoughts.

The European Language Portfolio

The European Language Portfolio is a system which enables students to maintain a record of their achievements and of their progress in language learning. It can include CEF self-assessment checklists for different languages, test or examination certificates and comments and feedback from teachers for each of the languages that they are studying. Students are able to update the European Language Portfolio for each language they are studying as they progress though school and university and it provides a record for themselves and their employers of what they have done and of what they can do in a number of different languages.

The Challenges Portfolio

Students keep a *portfolio* while they are studying *Challenges 1*. Look at page 75 of *Challenges 1* for an example. You will notice that students produce a piece of written work, an e-mail about their story, for their *portfolio*.

> **Task:** *Have a look through* **Challenges 1** *and make a note of all the For Your Portfolio sections. What different tasks do students do for their portfolios? Note down four ways you could help students to manage and organise their portfolios.*

Over to you!

Here is an idea to help you develop your understanding of the CEF of Reference for Languages

TP Look at the website for the CEF on *www.coe.int/T/E/Cultural_Co-operation/education/Languages/Language_Policy/Co* and find the sections which describe learners at A2 level. Focus on the self-assessment grid for the different language skills. Think how you might adapt these and use them with your students. Note down your ideas in your *teacher portfolio*.

www.challenges-elt.com

Coping with learning difficulties

Dyslexia

The word *dyslexia* comes from two Greek words meaning *difficulty* and *word* – hence the meaning of *difficulty with words*.

From this definition we might well consider any reader who has had opportunity over time to learn to read and write but who hasn't made effective progress *dyslexic*. Many learners and indeed parents, are comforted by the word *dyslexia* since it gives a name to a problem. Of course it is possible that students with general learning difficulties could also have delayed development in reading.

Although we acknowledge that there is ongoing debate regarding the term *dyslexia*, we will use it in this section for ease of reading.

What is dyslexia?

Dyslexia describes a problem with information processing difficulty with a core problem of dealing with the sound system of language (the phonology). Spoken language makes use of a set number of sounds. In communicating these are produced in a sequence at a very fast rate in order to communicate. The listener has to distinguish sound differences in a word, and keep them in the sequence produced by the speaker. In this way the listener is able to make sense of the words. A dyslexic student has difficulty in understanding how the sound system is organised. This does not only mean a difficulty in dealing with individual words but also grammatical structures, since words must be organised in a certain way to make comprehensible sentences.

Learning to differentiate sounds into segments and blending them to make words is not a natural process when it comes to *written* language. The reader or writer has to be able to understand and manipulate an alphabet system at a very efficient level. Most dyslexic students develop a degree of competency at the spoken word level but the competency may not be sufficient to allow for proficient reading and writing.

Learning to use an alphabet system

To learn to read a language such as English, the student must know how the set of sounds in a language are represented by an alphabet system. This will include learning how *patterns* of letters symbolise the different language sounds. This is not a straightforward matter since in English we have only twenty-six letters with over forty-two sounds. The same pattern of letters can represent different sounds. For example the pattern *ow* has a different sound in the words *cow* / kəʊ / and *snow* / snəʊ.

On the other hand, different letters, or letter combinations, can represent the same sound. The word *red*, for example, shares the same sound as the word *bread* but the sounds are represented by different letter patterns. The alphabet works like a code and so unknown written words must be read by segmenting the word into their letter patterns that represent certain sounds. The sounds represented by these segments then need to be blended together again to make sense. The opposite process happens in spelling. A dyslexic person will have varying degrees of difficulty in segmenting* and blending* skills and therefore in correctly matching sounds with their written symbols.

*segmenting: dividing something into parts that are different from each other

*blending: combining different things

Areas of difficulty that a dyslexic student may face

A student with dyslexia is likely to have difficulties in the following developmental areas:

▶ Listening comprehension

▶ Learning new vocabulary

▶ Reading fluency

▶ Writing

▶ Understanding syntax

▶ Confidence

A student may have difficulties in some or all of these areas and they will have developed their own way of dealing with any barriers to learning. Each person has his or her own pattern of strengths. Once the teacher gets to know the class it is important to use the strengths to support learning. This teaching approach will benefit all the students, since all students are uncertain and challenged in learning a new language.

Strategies for support of a dyslexic student

Teachers can reduce the barriers to learning of a dyslexic student by using a range of teaching strategies. However, it will be impossible to address all the learning needs of such students. Your main aim should be to help your students fully access your lesson, rather than solve their reading difficulties.

The following two tables give strategies that can be applied in every language class. Specific suggestions are made for the use of aspects of the ***Challenges Modules***. It is important to remember that each individual student will have their own pattern of strengths and needs and dyslexia is best understood as being on a continuum from mild to severe difficulties. The general strategies can be used to support learning across the lesson not just to meet the specific needs mentioned.

1. Strategies relating to difficulties of memory, organisation and stamina

SPECIFIC DIFFICULITES EXPERIENCED BY SOME DYSLEXIC STUDENTS	GENERAL STRATEGIES	SPECIFIC SUGGESTIONS FOR *CHALLENGES* MATERIAL
Processing of sequential information	Present spoken and written materials in a very clear, structured form. Avoid lengthy spoken explanations.	A dyslexic student may need support to use the sequence patterns of grammar tables.
Remembering what has been said long enough to understand the meaning	Visual support of new ideas helps a student to grasp ideas presented. Speak at an even pace and always check that a student has understood. S/he may want to avoid attention so a teacher needs to check in a sensitive, non-obvious way.	Whenever possible allow the dyslexic student time to read a passage several times before listening to a tape.
Tiredness: dyslexic students have to work harder than the average to process information	Do not overload with too many new structures at any one time. Understand lapses in attention as signs of fatigue and not laziness.	Consider giving less homework to a dyslexic student than the rest of the class.
Organisation: some dyslexic students have difficulty organising work and ideas on paper	Whenever possible provide the student with structure, for example a table to complete. Ensure that a student is sure of what s/he needs to do for homework before leaving the class.	The *Practice* sections of *Challenges* are well-structured writing exercises. To be most effective for a dyslexic student the teacher should go through some answers with the student.

2. Strategies relating to difficulties with reading, writing and confidence

SPECIFIC DIFFICULITES EXPERIENCED BY SOME DYSLEXIC STUDENTS	GENERAL STRATEGIES	SPECIFIC SUGGESTIONS FOR *CHALLENGES* MATERIAL
Pace and accuracy of reading	Do not ask a dyslexic student to read in front of class unless s/he volunteers. Check that the student has understood what was read. Minimise the amount of reading a student must undertake without good preparation of new words.	In pair work, pair a dyslexic student up with one who reads well but who is sensitive to the needs of others. The *Get Ready* section of *Challenges* is a key way to prepare the context for the reading material. Check that the student understands the meaning of the key words.
Self-esteem and confidence	All learners need to experience success. Teachers can build confidence by modelling (i.e. demonstrating) examples of how to use new material. It may be possible to have a class discussion about strengths and talents and difficulties we *all* experience in some way.	The *Sentence Builder* section of *Challenges* is an excellent means of teacher modelling.
Quality and quantity of writing	Help to prevent too many spelling errors by providing the student with a spelling card relevant to the writing task set. (A card with spellings listed that are most useful to the task.) Do not ask the student to copy much from the board. Consider whether work needs to be written in order to achieve the learning target. A pupil may be able to get through a lot more work if the outcome can be oral.	The writing and spelling tasks of *Challenges* may be very demanding for a dyslexic student. Working in pairs with a writing partner can help.

Photocopiable Activities: Teacher's notes

Resource 1: Find your partner
Aims: To practise countries and nationalities.
Interaction: Groups of up to fifteen students.
Materials: One card per student.
Instructions: 1 Hand out the cards and tell Ss not to show theirs to anyone else. Explain that the card tells Ss who they are, where they are from and who they are looking for. Ss must find that person by going up to others and asking: *Is your name … ? Are you from … ?* Ss answer *Yes it is / I am* or *No, my name's / I'm from … .* **2** When all the Ss have found who they want to find, they sit down. **3** Follow up by putting Ss into two groups. Ss work together to try to remember the names and nationalities of all the people in the other group. Elicit answers: *His name's … He's from …* and award points for correct answers and correct grammar.

Resource 2: John's family tree
Aims: To practise family relationship vocabulary.
Interaction: Pairs.
Materials: One family tree per pair. One set of clues per pair (or one per group – see optional activity).
Instructions: 1 Hand out the family tree and tell Ss they are going to fill in all the missing names by reading clues. **2 Either: a** Hand out the clues numbered so that the Ss can easily complete the family tree **OR b** Cut up the clues and hand them out without numbers to make it more challenging **OR c** Stick the clues around the room. The Ss still work together to complete the tree but must find the clues, read and remember them one at a time, returning to their desk to fill in the tree. This is more fun but also much noisier. **3** Follow up by asking questions about the family: *Who is Carole's father?* etc. Ss put up their hands to answer and win points for correct answers.

Resource 3: Spot the differences
Aims: To revise classroom objects and prepositions of place.
Interaction: Pairs.
Materials: One set of materials, A or B, per student.
Instructions: 1 Put the Ss into pairs. Hand out the material to each student and tell them not to show their partner. Make sure Ss know what each object in the picture is. **2** Student A says one thing about their picture. Student B tells them if their picture is different, e.g. A: *A bin is under the board.* B: *In my picture, a cupboard is under the board.* **3** Ss continue until they have found all ten differences. **4** When students have finished, check the answers as a class.

Resource 4: What time is … ?
Aims: To revise school subjects and times.
Interaction: Pairs.
Materials: One set of materials, A or B, per student.
Instructions: 1 Put Ss into pairs. Hand out the materials and tell Ss not to show their partner. **2** Tell Ss that they must ask their partner about the four missing subjects and complete their timetable. **3** Student A starts by asking: *What time is Science?* B answers: *At quarter to ten on Monday, at twenty past one on Tuesday, at five past two on Tuesday …* etc. **4** When finished, Ss compare completed timetables to make sure they are the same. **5** Monitor and note errors with times, pronunciation of school subjects and prepositions of time (*on / at*).

Resource 5: What is this?
Aims: To revise *this, that, these* and *those*.
Interaction: Pairs or small groups.
Materials: One set of cards cut up per group.
Instructions: 1 Put one set of cards, face down in a pile on the desk in front of the group. **2** One student picks up the top card and shows it to the others. Depending on the picture, the student asks: *What's this / that? What are these / those?* The other Ss have to answer: *This / that is a … These / Those are … .* **3** Monitor and make sure Ss are asking and answering correctly. **4** At the end of the activity, elicit questions and answers with the whole class.

Resource 6: Double dictation
Aims: To revise articles, descriptions and prepositions of place.
Interaction: Pairs.
Materials: One set of materials, A or B, per person. One set of pictures per pair.
Instructions: 1 Put Ss into pairs. If you don't mind a lot of noise, this can work well if Ss are partnered with someone from the other side of the room. **2** Tell Ss that they are going to dictate their part of the description to their partner who must write it down. Ss cannot show each other their paper – it should be a listening task. **3** When Ss have finished, give them the two pictures and ask which one they were describing. (Answer: picture 1.) Together they must try to find six differences between the text and the other picture.

Resource 7: What can you do with a broken arm?
Aims: To practise *can* and *can't*.
Interaction: Groups of three.
Materials: One copy of the material per student. Also needed: selotape, scissors, ruler, envelope, pencil, rubber for each group.
Instructions: 1 Pre-teach: *broken*. Hand out the material and read through the box next to the picture with the whole class. Tell Ss to write *can* or *can't* in the column marked *I think I … .* **2** Students compare their answers in groups of three. **3** Tell Ss to pack their books in their bags but to keep the resource, pens and pencil cases on the table. **4** Hand out the other items that Ss need (envelope, ruler, scissors, selotape and rubber). **5** Name each student in the groups A, B or C and tell them to imagine that one arm is broken – the one that they write with – and they cannot use it at all because it hurts. Each student in turn tries to do the things written in the survey and notes whether they can or can't do them well. **6** When all Ss have finished, elicit what they can or can't do.

Resource 8: Make a question
Aims: To practise question forms.
Interaction: Groups of three.
Materials: One copy of the resource, cut up, per group.
Instructions: 1 Place the question words in a pile, face down on the desk in front of the Ss and tell them not to look at them. **2** Ss divide the other cards equally between themselves. **3** One student in each group now picks up a question word from the pile and tries to put it with one of their endings to make a question. If this is possible, they lay the cards on the table and ask the question to the other Ss in the group. If they can't make a meaningful question, they put the question word at the bottom of the pile and the next student takes a turn. **4** The game continues until one student has made questions from all five of their cards. **5** Monitor and correct question forms.

Resource 9: Who is it?
Aims: To practise describing people using *to be* and *to have* in questions replies.
Interaction: Pairs.
Materials: Two sets of cards per pair, cut up.
Instructions: 1 Place one set of cards face down in a pile on the desk and lay the second set out so that all character cards are visible. Try to mix up the men and women so that it is a little more difficult. **2** One student picks up a card from the pile but doesn't show it to their partner. The second student must find out who it is by asking yes / no questions. Elicit ideas of questions that could be asked (e.g. *Is it a man? Is he tall? Has he got a tattoo?*). **3** As the student finds out information, they turn over the cards which are obviously wrong until there is only one card left. **4** Ss swap roles and a new card is chosen. Monitor and note errors in question formation and go over these at the end.

Resource 10: Whose food is it?
Aims: To practise possessive *'s* and revise food vocabulary.
Interaction: Groups of four.
Materials: One set of materials per group, cut up.
Instructions: 1 Hand out a name card to each student. Ss lay these on the table for everyone to see. **2** Hand out a meal card to each

person but tell them not to show them to each other. **3** Put the food cards on the table for everyone to see. **4** Ss have to find out whose food each item is by asking questions, e.g. *Are these Mark's potatoes?* If the person who is Mark has carrots on their meal card, they reply *yes* and the person who asks the question takes the card. If not, they say *no* and the next student asks a different question. The winner is the person with the most food cards at the end of the game. **5** Monitor and correct where necessary.

Resource 11: How well do you know your partner?
Aims: To practise present simple daily routines in first person and third person form.
Interaction: Individually then in pairs.
Materials: One set of the materials per student.
Instructions: 1 Tell Ss to complete the information for themselves in the column marked *Me*. **2** Partner Ss with someone who they are not sitting next to, so that they can't have seen what their 'partner' has written. Tell Ss to guess what their partner wrote and write the guesses in the second column. **3** Ss now sit with their partner but don't show each other what they wrote. Each student in turn tells the other what they think: *You get up at 7 o'clock* and the partner says whether it is right or wrong. The Ss write a tick or cross in the fourth column and the correct answer. **4** Elicit answers from Ss in open class so that they use first and third person forms in their answers e.g. *I get up at 7 and Anna gets up at 7.15.*

Resource 12: Cross the river
Aims: To practise present simple question forms.
Interaction: Small groups of three or four.
Materials: One set of the materials (and a dice) for each group.
Instructions: 1 Tell Ss that they are going to try to get across a river by forming questions. **2** One student throws the dice. The number determines whether the question starts with *where, what* etc. **3** The same student throws again to get the next word in the sentence (if they throw a 1 on their second throw, they fall in the river and have to stop their turn). **4** The student continues until they have either a) completed a sentence – in which case they write it down, or b) landed on a word that would make a sentence ungrammatical, e.g. *When does your friends …* then it is the turn of another student. **5** Continue until all Ss have had four or five turns. The winner is the student with the most questions written down. **6** After the activity, go over the question forms with the class.

Resource 13: Surveys
Aims: To practise questions and adverbs of frequency.
Interaction: Groups of five.
Materials: One survey card per student. One TV survey card per group as an example.
Instructions: 1 Put the Ss into five groups and hand out a TV survey card to one member of each group. This student asks the questions to the other members of the group. Elicit answers from each group. **2** Hand out a survey card to each student, all the Ss of each group must have the same survey card. Tell the Ss to work together to think of six questions similar to those asked about TV. Monitor and correct where necessary. **3** When finished, change the groups so that there are now new groups made up of one student from each of the original groups. **4** Each student in turn asks their questions and notes the answers from the other Ss in the group. **5** Ss go back to their original groups and compare answers. From these they give results from the class as a whole, e.g. *Seven people watch TV every day. Twelve people have a TV in their bedroom.*

Resource 14: Find the differences
Aims: To practise *there is / are* and prepositions of location with town vocabulary.
Interaction: Pairs.
Materials: One set of the materials, A or B, per student.
Instructions: 1 Hand out the material to each student and tell them not to show their partner **2** Tell Ss they have to try to find six differences between their pictures by describing the things in them and where they are, e.g. A *In my picture there's a car park.* B *In my picture there are two car parks.* **3** Monitor and note any errors. **4** When students have finished, check the answers with the class.

Resource 15: What's the question?
Aims: Practise question forms using *There is / are, How many* and *Why*.
Interaction: Pairs/groups of four.
Materials: One set of materials A or B, per student.
Instructions: 1 Put Ss in pairs, hand out one copy of the resource A or B to each pair. Tell them to look at the first box on their paper which has the answers to some questions. They have to try to work out what the questions are. If they get them right, they score the number of points written and the students with the most points are the winners. **2** Allow Ss five minutes to work out the questions and write them down. **3** Join As and Bs together in a group of four and tell them not to show each other their resource. **4** Ss tell each other the questions they wrote down and say that the other group has the correct questions in the second box on their resource. **5** Ss keep a total of how many points the other side scores and add it up at the end. The winning group is the one with the most points. **6** Elicit all the correct questions and any problems Ss had while doing the activity.

Resource 16: What are they doing?
Aims: To practise present continuous.
Interaction: Pairs.
Materials: One set of the materials, A or B, per student.
Instructions: 1 Hand out the material to each student and tell them not to show their partner. **2** Tell Ss they have a picture of the same place and the same people but that the people are doing or wearing different things. They have to try to find six differences between their pictures by describing the people in them and what they are doing, e.g. A *The woman is wearing a dress.* B *In my picture she is wearing jeans and a T-shirt.* **3** Monitor and note any errors. **4** Check the differences as a whole class.

Resource 17: Memory game
Aims: To practise *was / were* in questions and answers.
Interaction: Pairs.
Materials: One set of materials, A or B, per pair.
Instructions: 1 Draw a picture on the board or show Ss a flashcard. Allow Ss to see the picture and then rub it out or hide it. Tell Ss they are going to ask questions about the picture using *was / were*. Elicit ideas and write on the board, e.g. *How many people were there? Was there a dog? What colour was the car?* etc. **2** Hand out the pictures to Ss and tell them they have two minutes to look at them and remember as much detail as possible. Tell Ss that, if there is anything in their picture they don't know the word for, they should ask now. **3** Ss swap pictures with their partner and look at their partner's picture. Ss can either write questions down or simply say them. When ready, Ss take it in turns to test their partner's memory of what was in their picture using a variety of question forms as in part 1. Tell Ss that when they answer, they should give full sentences, i.e. *Yes, there were two boys. No, there wasn't a bank.* **4** Monitor and note errors.

Resource 18: Consequences
Aims: To practise past simple on the topic of explorers.
Interaction: Ss work alone or in pairs. Materials are passed around the class.
Materials: One set of materials per student or pair.
Instructions: 1 Practise expanding sentences from cues so that Ss know what to do. Write on the board: *Yesterday I / play tennis* and elicit the full sentence (*Yesterday, I played tennis*). **2** Hand out the material and tell Ss to read through all the sections to make sure they understand everything. If there are any problems, go through them with the whole class before the activity starts. **3** Elicit how to expand the words given into a grammatically correct form and then tell Ss to complete the first box only and to fold over the paper so that what they have written is hidden. **4** Ss pass their paper to the student on their left and, without looking at what was written before, complete the second section and again fold over the paper. **5** Continue until all sections have been completed and then Ss open out the paper to read the story. Allow Ss to read out any particularly funny stories to the whole class.

Resource 19: Truth or lie?
Aims: To practise past simple positives, questions and negatives.
Interaction: Groups of four.
Materials: One set of materials per group, cut up.
Instructions: 1 Tell the Ss they are going to make sentences about things they did or didn't do in the past. The other members of the group must decide whether they are telling the truth or not. Say to Ss: *Last night, I watched a film on TV.* Elicit questions that they might ask you, e.g. *What was the film? What channel was it on? What happened?* Ask Ss if they think you are telling the truth or not and tell them if they are right. 2 Hand out the materials in two piles, face down on the desk in front of the Ss. The first student in each group picks up a *time card* and an *event card* and makes a sentence, either positive or negative. 3 Others in the group ask questions to see if they think the student is telling the truth. Continue, with different Ss saying the sentences in turn until all the cards have gone. 4 Elicit things Ss said and how many times they tricked their partners.

Resource 20: Find out
Aims: To practise past simple questions.
Interaction: Groups of up to eight.
Materials: One card per student.
Instructions: 1 Ss look at the piece of information that they have and try to work out the questions they will need to ask to find out the rest of the information. 2 Ss stand up and mingle in their groups of eight and ask and answer and fill in their information. Ss ask questions such as: *Where was this person born?* Monitor and note errors in question formation. 3 Ss ask and answer the eight questions as a whole class.

Resource 21: Who's the best?
Aims: To practise comparatives.
Interaction: Pairs.
Materials: One set of cards, cut up for each pair – ten cards each.
Instructions: 1 Go through the nouns written on the cards and elicit the adjective corresponding to each. 2 Put Ss in pairs and give ten cards to each student. Ss must have the cards face down in front of them. 3 In pairs, Ss decide who is going first. The first person nominates one of the categories on the card. Each student takes the top card of their pile and puts it on the table. The student with the highest score for that category must then make a sentence, e.g. *David is more intelligent than James* in order to win the cards. 4 The winner then chooses the category for the next round. 5 At the end of the game, Ss count up how many cards they have got. 6 Ss can then repeat the game.

Resource 22: What's the top answer?
Aims: To practise superlatives.
Interaction: Whole class.
Materials: One set of cards, cut up.
Instructions: 1 Put the class into two groups and choose one person from each group to come out to the front. 2 Choose the first card from the list and read out the heading as a question, e.g. *What is the best animal to have as a pet?* The first of the two to raise their hand gives their answer. If this is the top answer (dog), their group plays. If not, the other student can try to choose an answer that has more points. 3 The playing group take it in turn to guess the words on the card. If they find all the choices, they win 100 points. If they make a mistake, i.e they guess an animal which is not on the card, it passes over to the other group. The other group have one chance to name one of the missing choices. If they manage it, they win all the points. If not, the first group wins all the points. 4 Continue until you have used all twelve cards. The winning group is the one with the most points. 5 Ss then work in pairs trying to remember what was on the cards and write sentences, e.g. *Football is the most exciting sport.*

Resource 23: Island rules
Aims: To practise modals of obligation or prohibition (*must / mustn't, can, / can't*).
Interaction: Groups of eleven / groups of two or three.

Materials: One rule card per student, one island card per pair / group of three.
Instructions: 1 Hand out the rules cards to each student and tell them not to show theirs to anyone else. 2 Students mingle in groups of eleven and tell each other their rules. Ss cannot write anything down, they must just listen and try to remember. 3 When Ss have spoken to everyone in their groups, they get into pairs or groups of four. 4 Hand out the island card. Ss work together to remember what all the rules were and to complete the gapped sentences. 5 When Ss have written all the rules, they take the letters with asterisks below them and use these to find the name of the island (elephant). 6 *Optional follow up:* Ss draw a map of their own island showing geographical features and then write a set of rules to go with it. This can be quite a major project with Ss thinking of major sports, languages, industries and any other features that revise vocabulary from earlier in the book.

Resource 24: What do you do well?
Aims: To practise adverbs of manner.
Interaction: Either groups of four or five sitting **OR** whole class mingling.
Materials: One card per student for mingling **OR** one set of cards cut up per group.
Instructions: (**Mingling**) 1 Hand out one card per student. Ss stand up and ask as many other Ss their question as they can, writing the answers in their notebooks. Encourage Ss to give full answers and justify them with examples, e.g. *I can do running easily. I won the 100m in the last school sports competition.* 2 Ss sit down in groups of three or four and compare information. 3 Elicit feedback in open class.
(**Groups**) 1 Place the cards face down on the desk in front of the Ss. One student in each group picks up the first card and each of the others in turn answers the question. Ss justify their answers and try to talk together for a minute for each card. 2 The next student picks up the next card and the process continues. 3 Monitor and note errors and interesting answers. 4 Do any corrections with the whole class.

Resource 25: Plan a holiday
Aims: To practise *going to* for future plans.
Interaction: Groups of three or four.
Materials: One set per group. Dice and counters for each group.
Instructions: 1 Tell Ss they are going to plan a holiday and must find out seven things: 1. Where they are going 2. When they are going 3. How they are going to travel 4. Where they are going to stay 5. Who they are going with 6. How long they are going for and 7. What they are going to do. 2 To find out these things, they must land on a square on the board. They then note down what it says. If they have already got a *place* and land on another *place* square, they do not write anything and have to wait until their next turn. The winner is the first student in each group to get all seven pieces of information. 3 Ss play the game. When one student finishes, you can choose whether to let the others continue or to stop the activity. 4 Ss write down their holiday plans from the board game using *going to*, e.g. *I'm going to go to France. I'm going to travel by bike* etc. Elicit from the class what Ss know about their holidays. Correct any errors with *going to* as necessary. 5 Ss work together in their groups and decide which of their holidays is the best and why.

Resource 26: Whose is it?
Aims: To practise possessive adjectives.
Interaction: Pairs/small groups.
Materials: One set, cut up, per group.
Instructions: 1 Hand out the three *people* cards to each group and ask Ss to think about the people, and what they are like. Ss work together to make up a complete identity for the characters with a name, job, information about family, hobbies etc. Elicit ideas from each group in open class. 2 Hand out the *object* cards face down in a pile in front of the students. Ss pick up a card, one at a time and, as a group, decide who each object belongs to *It's / They're his / hers / theirs …* or they can use the names they made up in part 1: e.g. *It's John's.* 3 Elicit ideas and reasons from the Ss.

43

1: Find your partner

You are: David Prince **From:** The USA **You want to find:** Jose DeSilva from Portugal	**You are:** Jose DeSilva **From:** Portugal **You want to find:** Steve Davis from the United Kingdom	**You are:** Steve Davis **From:** The United Kingdom **You want to find:** Kamal Bey from Turkey
You are: Kamal Bey **From:** Turkey **You want to find:** Gabriel Crespo from Argentina	**You are:** Gabriel Crespo **From:** Argentina **You want to find:** Antonio Cruz from Spain	**You are:** Antonio Cruz **From:** Spain **You want to find:** Marie Distel from Canada
You are: Marie Distel **From:** Canada **You want to find:** Jean Delain from France	**You are:** Jean Delain **From:** France **You want to find:** Dan Gallagher from Ireland	**You are:** Dan Gallagher **From:** Ireland **You want to find:** Claire Hornsby from Australia
You are: Claire Hornsby **From:** Australia **You want to find:** Suzuki Yo from Japan	**You are:** Suzuki Yo **From:** Japan **You want to find:** Giancarlo Maldini from Italy	**You are:** Giancarlo Maldini **From:** Italy **You want to find:** Kasia Jaromin from Poland
You are: Kasia Jaromin **From:** Poland **You want to find:** Anna Federov from Russia	**You are:** Anna Federov **From:** Russia **You want to find:** Jose Borgas from Greece	**You are:** Jose Borges **From:** Greece **You want to find:** David Prince from the USA

2: John's family tree

1. Carole is my wife.
2. David is my brother.
3. Sue is my niece.
4. Fred is my nephew.
5. Hannah and James are my son and daughter.
6. Hannah and James and Fred and Sue are cousins.
7. David and Alison are husband and wife.
8. Bob is my father.
9. Emily is my mother.
10. Steven and Carole are brother and sister.
11. Emily and Kate are grandmothers.
12. Bob and Tom are grandfathers.

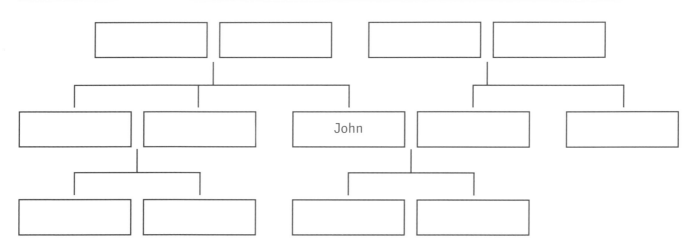

3: Spot the differences

Describe your room to your partner and listen to their description.
Find ten differences.

Describe your room to your partner and listen to their description.
Find ten differences.

PHOTOCOPIABLE

4: What time is ... ?

Complete your timetable. What time are these subjects?
    Science
    English
    History
    Music

A

	Monday	Tuesday	Wednesday	Thursday	Friday
9.00	Maths	?	Art	?	?
9.45	?	French	Art	?	?
10.55	Geography	?	?	Maths	Geography
11.35	Art	?	Geography	?	?
1.20	PE	Maths	PE	?	French
2.05	PE	Maths	PE	?	Maths

Complete your timetable. What time are these subjects?
    Maths
    Art
    French
    Geography

B

	Monday	Tuesday	Wednesday	Thursday	Friday
9.00	?	English	?	English	History
9.45	Science	?	?	English	History
10.55	?	History	French	?	?
11.35	?	Music	?	Music	English
1.20	PE	?	PE	Science	?
2.05	PE	?	PE	Science	?

5: What is this?

6: Double dictation

A: ----------------- of my mother. ----------------- . She is short, thin and blonde. ----------------- . The house is our house. ----------------- . The dog is small and dark. ----------------- . Behind my mum is a boy. ----------------- . He is tall and dark. ----------------- . He's a good friend.

B: This is a photo ----------------- . She is forty-nine years old. ----------------- . She is next to a house . ----------------- . Next to my mum is a dog. ----------------- . It isn't my dog. ----------------- . He's my brother. ----------------- . He is a student. ----------------- .

7: What can you do with a broken arm?

Imagine you have a broken arm.

In the table are some things that you want to do. But can you do them?

Write *can* if you think you can do them with a broken arm and *can't* if you think you can't do them.

	I think I ...	A	B	C
Open your bag and put your books on the table.				
Take a piece of paper from your notebook.				
Write your name on the paper.				
Use a ruler to draw a line across the paper.				
Cut along the line with a pair of scissors.				
Stick the two halves of paper together again with selotape.				
Draw a circle on the piece of paper.				
Rub out the circle with a rubber.				
Fold the paper in half.				
Put the paper into an envelope.				

8: Make a question

Who	Who	Who	Where	Where
Where	What	What	What	How many
How many	How many	How old	How old	How old

chairs are in the room?	

languages can you speak?	students are in the room?
is your teacher's name?	musical instruments can you play?
subject is at 11 o'clock on Tuesday?	are you from?
is the bin?	is Buenos Aires?
is your best friend?	is the person next to you?
can play guitar in his class?	is your teacher?
is his school?	are you?

9: Who is it?

10: Whose food is it?

Meal cards ✂

Name cards ✂

MARK	BELINDA	STEVE	EMMA

Food cards ✂

11: How well do you know your partner?

Complete the information about you in the first column.

	Me	My partner	✓/✗
I get up at … .			
I eat … for breakfast.			
I go to school by … . (how?)			
I leave home at … .			
I eat … for lunch.			
I get home at … .			
I start my homework at … .			
I watch … on television.			
I go to bed at … .			
On Saturdays I … .			
On Saturdays I go to bed at … .			
On Sundays I get up at … .			

12: Cross the river

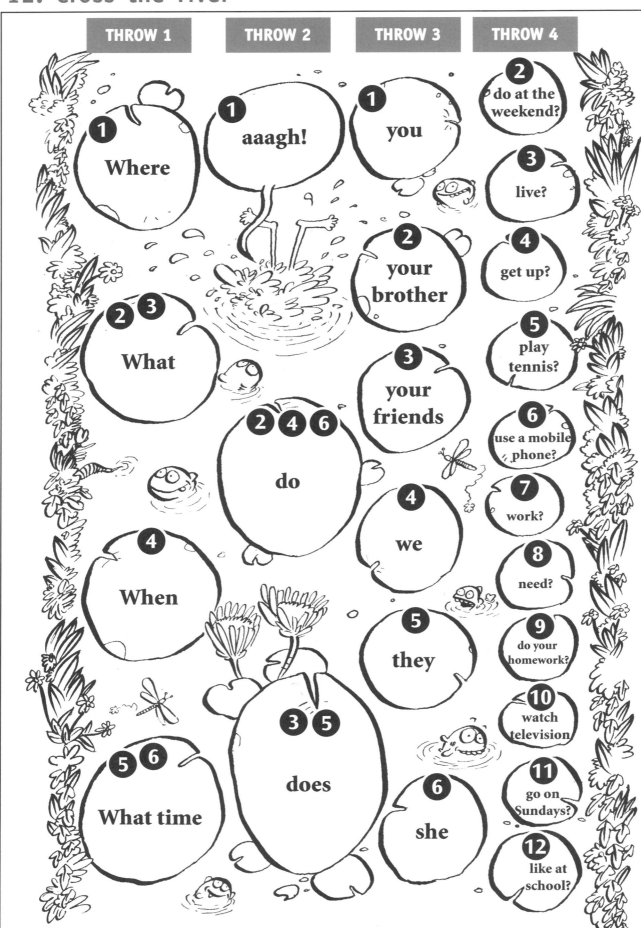

13: Surveys

TV

1. How often do you watch TV?
2. When do you watch TV?
3. Have you got a TV in your bedroom?
4. Do you watch TV in the morning?
5. Does your family watch TV together?
6. What's your favourite programme?

Free time

1. How often ...
2. What ...
3. Do you ...
4. Does your ...
5. Where ...
6. When ...

School

1. How often ...
2. What ...
3. Do you ...
4. Does your ...
5. Where ...
6. When ...

Sport

1. How often ...
2. What ...
3. Do you ...
4. Does your ...
5. Where ...
6. When ...

Food and drink

1. How often ...
2. What ...
3. Do you ...
4. Does your ...
5. Where ...
6. When ...

Daily routine

1. How often ...
2. What ...
3. Do you ...
4. Does your ...
5. Where ...
6. When ...

14: Find the differences

15 What's the question?

A

Points	Your answers. Can you make the questions?
100	There are thirty students in this class.
200	No, there isn't a television in this room.
500	Yes, there is some water on the desk.
1000	Because it's Saturday. (students / in school?)
5000	Because it's my birthday. (cake / table?)
10,000	Because it's hot and sunny. (coats / classroom?)

Points	These are B's question. Are they correct?
100	Is there a teacher in this room?
200	Is there any juice in your bag?
500	How many desks are there in this room?
1000	Why is there a pen on the / your desk?
5000	Why are there clouds in the sky?
10,000	Why aren't there any cars in the car park?

- -

B

Points	Your answers. Can you make the questions?
100	Yes, there is a teacher in this room.
200	No, there isn't any juice in my bag.
500	There are six desks in this room.
1000	Because I want to write. (pen / desk?)
5000	Because it isn't a nice day. (clouds / sky?)
10,000	Because the teachers like walking. (cars / car park?)

Points	These are B's questions. Are they correct?
100	How many students are there in this class?
200	Is there a television in this room?
500	Is there any water on the desk?
1000	Why aren't there any students in school?
5000	Why is there a cake on the table?
10,000	Why aren't there any coats in the classroom?

16: What are they doing?

Work with a partner. Find six differences.

Work with a partner. Find six differences.

PHOTOCOPIABLE

17: Memory game

18: Consequences

This is the story of the great Explorer called …

He/she / want / discover …

He/she / travel by

First place he/she / come to

He/she / see

He/she / meet

He/she / say

He/she / feel

He/she want

He/she …

At the end of the journey, he/she …

19: Truth or lie?

Time cards ✂

This morning	Last night	On Saturday morning	On Saturday evening
On Sunday morning	On Sunday afternoon	Last week	Last month
Last year	At Christmas	On my birthday	At the weekend
Last Friday	Last lesson	When I was twelve	In 2003

Event cards ✂

Do homework	Watch a film	Tidy my room	Play football
Do the washing up	Go to bed early	Use a computer	Go shopping
Go to the cinema	Buy new shoes	Phone my friend	Drink milk
Write a letter	Travel by plane	Meet a pop star	Be tired

20: Find out

✂

Name: **Winona Ryder** Born in (date): Born in (place): Went to acting school in: First film: Became famous after: Played .... in *Little Women*. Started acting classes when she was:	Name: Born in (date): **October 1971** Born in (place): Went to acting school in: First film: Became famous after: Played .... in *Little Women*. Started acting classes when she was:
Name: Born in (date): Born in (place): **Minnesota, USA** Went to acting school in: First film: Became famous after: Played .... in *Little Women*. Started acting classes when she was:	Name: Born in (date): Born in (place): Went to acting school in: **Petaluma** First film: Became famous after: Played .... in *Little Women*. Started acting classes when she was:
Name: Born in (date): Born in (place): Went to acting school in: First film: **Lucas** Became famous after: Played .... in *Little Women*. Started acting classes when she was:	Name: Born in (date): Born in (place): Went to acting school in: First film: Became famous after **Beetlejuice**. Played .... in *Little Women*. Started acting classes when she was:
Name: Born in (date): Born in (place): Went to acting school in: First film: Became famous after: Played **Jo** in *Little Women*. Started acting classes when she was:	Name: Born in (date): Born in (place): Went to acting school in: First film: Became famous after: Played .... in *Little Women*. Started acting classes when she was **twelve**.

21: Who's the best?

Name: Mary		Name: Colin		Name: David		Name: Gareth	
Intelligence	10	Intelligence	9	Intelligence	8	Intelligence	7
Looks	2	Looks	7	Looks	8	Looks	9
Money	4	Money	10	Money	6	Money	9
Fame	5	Fame	4	Fame	4	Fame	9
Popularity	3	Popularity	2	Popularity	8	Popularity	5

Name: Tim		Name: Dawn		Name: Rachel		Name: Steve	
Intelligence	6	Intelligence	5	Intelligence	4	Intelligence	3
Looks	5	Looks	10	Looks	8	Looks	2
Money	5	Money	6	Money	3	Money	7
Fame	3	Fame	8	Fame	6	Fame	6
Popularity	6	Popularity	7	Popularity	6	Popularity	8

Name: Mark		Name: Mandy		Name: Theresa		Name: Jill	
Intelligence	2	Intelligence	1	Intelligence	2	Intelligence	3
Looks	9	Looks	8	Looks	3	Looks	6
Money	5	Money	10	Money	5	Money	8
Fame	4	Fame	8	Fame	5	Fame	7
Popularity	6	Popularity	9	Popularity	6	Popularity	9

Name: Peter		Name: Hannah		Name: James		Name: Jean	
Intelligence	4	Intelligence	5	Intelligence	6	Intelligence	7
Looks	6	Looks	6	Looks	1	Looks	9
Money	8	Money	7	Money	5	Money	7
Fame	8	Fame	6	Fame	9	Fame	8
Popularity	5	Popularity	8	Popularity	6	Popularity	5

Name: Isabela		Name: Sean		Name: Pierce		Name: Al	
Intelligence	8	Intelligence	9	Intelligence	10	Intelligence	5
Looks	5	Looks	2	Looks	5	Looks	7
Money	8	Money	2	Money	9	Money	5
Fame	5	Fame	5	Fame	9	Fame	3
Popularity	8	Popularity	8	Popularity	1	Popularity	8

22: What's the top answer?

✂

Best animal for a pet	The most exciting sport	Most popular country for a holiday	Worst thing about school
1. Dog 2. Cat 3. Rabbit 4. Hamster 5. Horse 6. Parrot	1. Football 2. Skiing 3. Basketball 4. Boxing 5. Cycling 6. Rugby	1. Spain 2. France 3. Greece 4. Italy 5. USA 6. Britain	1. Homework 2. Exams 3. Games lessons 4. Uniforms 5. Bullies 6. Lessons
Most famous rock band	**The most expensive car**	**The best food**	**The nicest fruit**
1. Beatles 2. U2 3. Rolling Stones 4. Queen 5. Doors 6. Nirvana	1. Ferrari 2. Porsche 3. Lambourgini 4. Rolls Royce 5. Alfa Romeo 6. Mercedes Benz	1. Italian 2. Chinese 3. French 4. Indian 5. Japanese 6. Indonesian	1. Melon 2. Strawberry 3. Banana 4. Orange 5. Peach 6. Grape
The most popular film	**The biggest city in the world**	**The best day of the week**	**The most famous football team**
1. *Star Wars* 2. *Titanic* 3. *Jurassic Park* 4. *Harry Potter* 5. *James Bond*	1. Tokyo 2. Shanghai 3. Bejing 4. New York 5. Sao Paolo	1. Saturday 2. Friday 3. Sunday 4. Wednesday 5. Thursday	1. Real Madrid 2. Manchester United 3. Juventus 4. AC Milan 5. Barcelona

23: Island rules

You mustn't eat meat on Sundays.	You can't smoke in restaurants.
You can't play football in the mornings.	You mustn't wear shorts in the summer.
You must drive on the left.	You must go to the cinema once a week.
You must say hello to five people every day.	You can go to bed when you want.
You can sleep in lessons.	You can use mobile phones in exams.
You must drink milk for breakfast.	

Rules of _ _ _ _ _ _ _ _ _ island

You mustn't _ _ _ _ _ _ _ _ _ _ _ _ _ _ _ _ _ _ .
                           *

You can't _ _ _ _ _ _ _ _ _ _ _ _ _ _ _ _ _ _ .

You can't _ _ _ _ _ _ _ _ _ _ _ _ _ _ _ _ _ _ _ _ _ _ _ .
                                *

You mustn't _ _ _ _ _ _ _ _ _ _ _ _ _ _ _ _ _ _ _ _ _ _ _ _ .

You must _ _ _ _ _ _ _ _ _ _ _ _ _ _ _ _ .
                                *

You must _ _ _ _ _ _ _ _ _ _ _ _ _ _ _ _ _ _ _ _ .

You must _ _ _ _ _ _ _ _ _ _ _ _ _ _ _ _ _ _ _ _ _ _ _ _ _ _ _ _ .
                                    *

You can _ _ _ _ _ _ _ _ _ _ _ _ _ _ _ .
                 *   *

You can _ _ _ _ _ _ _ _ _ _ _ _ _ _ .
             *

You can _ _ _ _ _ _ _ _ _ _ _ _ _ _ _ .

You must _ _ _ _ _ _ _ _ _ _ _ _ _ _ _ .
                         *

24: What do you do well?

Tell me one thing you do well.	Tell me one thing you do badly.	Tell me one thing you do quickly.	Tell me one thing you do slowly.
Tell me one thing you do carefully.	Tell me one thing you do easily.	Tell me one thing you do perfectly.	Tell me one thing you do happily.
Who do you know that can play the guitar very well?	Who do you know that writes very badly?	Who do you know that dresses very nicely?	Who do you know that speaks English perfectly?
Who do you know that does their homework very carefully?	Who do you know that passes exams very easily?	Who do you know that runs very fast?	Who do you know that laughs very loudly?

25: Plan a holiday

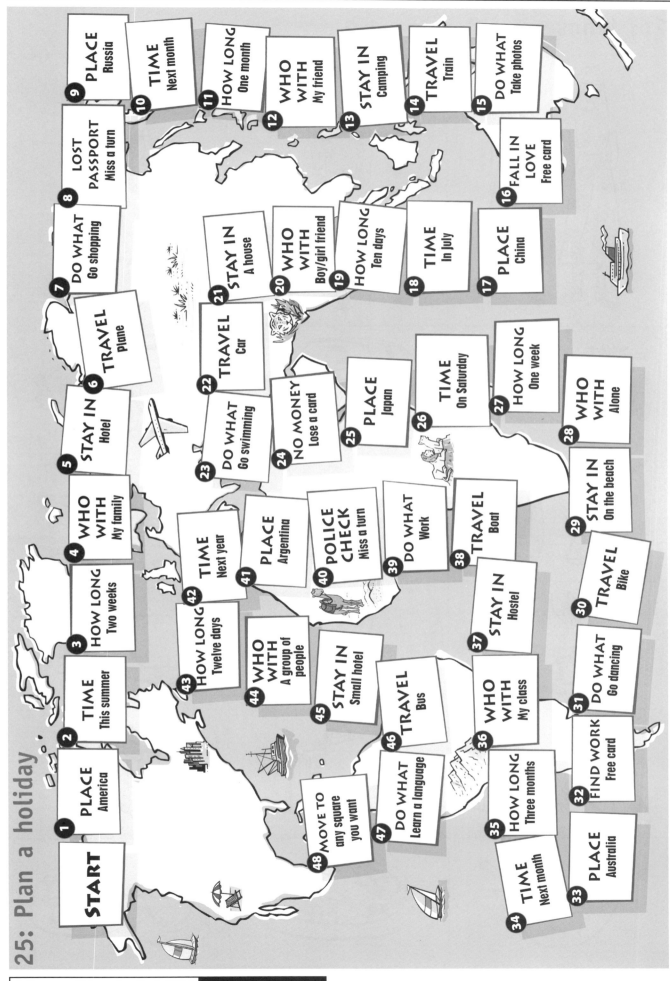

START

1 PLACE America
2 TIME This summer
3 HOW LONG Two weeks
4 WHO WITH My family
5 STAY IN Hotel
6 TRAVEL Plane
7 DO WHAT Go shopping
8 LOST PASSPORT Miss a turn
9 PLACE Russia
10 TIME Next month
11 HOW LONG One month
12 WHO WITH My friend
13 STAY IN Camping
14 TRAVEL Train
15 DO WHAT Take photos
16 FALL IN LOVE Free card
17 PLACE China
18 TIME In July
19 HOW LONG Ten days
20 WHO WITH Boy/girl friend
21 STAY IN A house
22 TRAVEL Car
23 DO WHAT Go swimming
24 NO MONEY Lose a card
25 PLACE Japan
26 TIME On Saturday
27 HOW LONG One week
28 WHO WITH Alone
29 STAY IN On the beach
30 TRAVEL Bike
31 DO WHAT Go dancing
32 FIND WORK Free card
33 PLACE Australia
34 TIME Next month
35 HOW LONG Three months
36 WHO WITH My class
37 STAY IN Hostel
38 TRAVEL Boat
39 DO WHAT Work
40 POLICE CHECK Miss a turn
41 PLACE Argentina
42 TIME Next year
43 HOW LONG Twelve days
44 WHO WITH A group of people
45 STAY IN Small hotel
46 TRAVEL Bus
47 DO WHAT Learn a language
48 MOVE TO any square you want

26: Whose is it?

Get Ready Test

Vocabulary

1 Nationalities
Put the letters in the correct order.

1. t u n i s l a a A r
_____

2. k r e e G
_____

3. a n d i C n a a
_____

4. i l r h s
_____

5. r h n c F e
_____

6. t n a a l i l
_____

7. e a n s e p a J
_____

8. h o s P l i
_____

9. t s o e e r u g P u
_____ ___

10. n s S i a h p
_____

☐ / 10

2 Numbers
Complete the crossword.
Write the numbers as words:

Across
2. 12
5. 14

Down
1. 60
3. 8
4. 90

☐ / 5

3 Family
Complete the sentences.

1. Jack and Claire are husband and w...............
2. Bob and Carole are brother and s...............
3. Steve and Debbie are uncle and a...............
4. Tom and Karen are son and d...............
5. Your mother and father are your p...............
6. Sally and Terry are niece and n...............
7. Colin and Daria are grandfather and g...............

☐ / 7

4 Months
Put the letters in the correct order to make months. Then put the months in order.

1. YAM ___ ___ ___
2. TOROECB ___ ___ ___ ___ ___ ___ ___
3. RAPIL ___ ___ ___ ___ ___
4. UJYL ___ ___ ___ ___
5. BYERAUFR ___ ___ ___ ___ ___ ___ ___ ___

☐ / 5

5 School subjects
Complete the words.

1. A ___ ___ ___
2. ___ ___ ___ ___ G R A ___ ___ ___ ___
3. ___ ___ ___ ___ I C
4. S ___ ___ ___ ___ ___ C ___
5. H ___ ___ ___ ___ O R ___

☐ / 5

Grammar

6 Verb *to be*
Complete the sentences with the verb *to be* in the correct form.

I [1]............... English, I'm American.
[2]............... she Italian? Yes, she [3]............... .
[4]............... they from Poland? No they [5]............... .
What [6]............... your name?
Where [7]............... you from?
[8]............... I in this class?
He [9]............... a student, he's a teacher.
[10]............... your teacher English?

☐ / 10

7 Subject pronouns, object pronouns and possessive adjectives

my (x 2)	him	he	our (x 4)	she
his	its	they	her	I	their	we

Complete the text with the words in the box.

¹.............. name is Jose. ².............. am at school. ³.............. brother is a student. ⁴.............. is tall. ⁵.............. are from Argentina. This is a photo of ⁶.............. house. ⁷.............. mother is in front of the house. ⁸.............. name is Juanita. ⁹.............. is a teacher. This is ¹⁰.............. father. ¹¹.............. name is Diego. This is ¹².............. dog. ¹³.............. name is Tommy. Behind my mother are two girls. ¹⁴.............. are from England. ¹⁵.............. names are Sonia and Kelly.

☐ / 15

8 Prepositions of place
Make sentences about the room. Use the words in the box.

in (x 2)	between	in front of	under
	next to	on	behind

1. radio / cupboard ....
2. bin / board ....
3. plant / window ....
4. board / window ....
5. plant / bookcase ....
6. books / bookcase ....
7. window / plant ....
8. blackboard / window – cupboard ....

☐ / 8

9 Imperatives
Complete the sentences. Use the words in the box.

Sit down	Speak	Close	Don't watch	Write

1. .... the window, it's cold!
2. .... TV every evening!
3. .... the sentences in your notebook.
4. .... English in class.
5. .... on your chair!

☐ / 5

10 *this*, *that*, *these*, *those*
Complete the sentences. Use *this*, *that*, *these* or *those*.

1. Is .... your bike over there?
2. Look here. .... is a photo of my family.
3. .... computer games over there are my favourites.
4. Come here and look at .... They are my new CDs.

☐ / 4

11 Articles
Complete the sentences with *a*, *an* or *the*.

1. I'm ..... student.
2. This is ..... photo of my school.
3. ..... man next to me is my father.
4. My brother is ..... tall, thin boy.
5. John is ..... good friend.
6. ..... woman in this photo is my aunt.
7. Where's my dog? He's in ..... garden.
8. My birthday is on ..... 15th July.

☐ / 8

Sentence Builder

12 Write the three sentences as one sentence.

1. My mother is a woman. My mother is tall. My mother is from France.

....

2. My teacher is a man. My teacher is old. My teacher is English.

....

3. My friend is a girl. My friend is blonde. My friend is from London.

....

☐ / 3

Total ☐ / 85

Module 1 Test

Vocabulary

1 Abilities
What can they do? Write a sentence for each picture.

1. He can a .... **2.** ....

3. .... **4.** ....

5. .... **6.** ....

☐ / 6

2 Opinion adjectives
Complete the sentences.

1. A: Do you like rap?   B: Yeah, it's c __ __ __ !

2. I like photography, it's really
i __ __ __ __ __ __ __ __ __ __ __ .

3. Brad Pitt is very g __ __ __ l __ __ __ __ __ __ !

4. A: Do you like rock music? B: Well, it's o __ __ __ .

☐ / 4

Grammar

3 Can
Tick (✓) the correct sentences. Correct the wrong
(✗) sentences.

e.g. Can Jenny ride a bike? ✓ I ~~'m~~ can play tennis. ✗

1. My mother isn't can use a computer.

....

2. What musical instrument you can play?

....

3. Where can I ride a horse?

....

4. What is you can cook?

....

5. They no can speak French.

....

6. You can't sing.

....

7. Can you play football? Yes, I'm can.

....

8. Can you paint? No, I can.

....

☐ / 8

4 Question words
Put the words in the correct order.

1. aunt How your is old?

....

2. is from mother your Where?

....

3. languages What speak you can?

....

4. your Italy Are from friends?

....

5. How family men in are your many?

....

6. What's subject your favourite?

....

7. is Where bin the?

....

8. this is How book old?

....

9. next Who window to is the the boy?

....

10. guitar How many the students can play?

....

☐ / 10

Sentence Builder

5 Join the two sentences. Use *and* or *but*.

1. I can swim. I can play chess.

....

2. I can sing. I can't act.

....

3. I'm into computers. I'm not into music.

....

4. I'm interested in maths. I like history.

....

5. I can speak French. I can't speak Spanish.

....

6. This is my computer. These are my computer
games.

....

☐ / 6

Key Expressions

**6 Look at the <u>underlined</u> words. Some are wrong.
Correct the mistakes.**

Are you interested [1]<u>into</u> Rap music? ....

No, I'm not. It's really [2]<u>fantastic</u>. ....

What are you [3]<u>into</u>? ....

I'm interested [4]<u>of</u> maths ....

Are you [5]<u>in</u> films? ....

Yes. The Harry Potter film is fantastic. It's
really [6]<u>boring</u>! ....

☐ / 6

Total ☐ / 40

Module 2 Test

Vocabulary

1 **Food, sport, appearance, clothes**
Add three words for each heading.

Food	Sport	Clothes
chicken	football	dress

/ 9

Grammar

2 *to be / to have*
Complete these sentences with the correct form of *to be* or *to have*. All sentences are positive.

1. I .... long hair.
2. My sister .... tall and thin.
3. My parents .... overweight.
4. You .... a tattoo.
5. We .... young.
6. My brother .... dark hair.
7. She .... blue eyes.
8. My friends .... a dog.

/ 8

3 *to be / to have*
Make questions and negatives with the verbs *to be* or *to have*.

1. your mother / young? ....
2. my sister / not / long hair ....
3. you / blue eyes? ....
4. he / not / fat ....
5. they / not / old ....
6. your parents / old? ....
7. we / not / blonde hair ....

/ 7

4 **Possessive 's**
Put an apostrophe (') in the correct place(s) in these sentences.

1. Johns brothers are tall.
2. He is in the mens swimming team.
3. Steves eyes are blue and Paulas eyes are green.
4. My girlfriends parents are tall and thin.
5. Is that Jamess photo?
6. The girls hockey team is very good.

/ 6

Sentence Builder

5 Join these sentences to make ONE sentence.

1. My mother is tall. My mother is slim.
   ....
2. That boy has got tattoos. That boy has got a pony tail.
   ....
3. Drew Barrymore has got blonde hair. Drew Barrymore has got blue eyes.
   ....
4. My parents are short. My parents are overweight.
   ....

/ 4

Key Expressions

6 Put these words into the correct place in the text.

it's	too	hard
how	easy	they're

[1]................. are things?
Not [2]................. bad.
How is the steak?
[3]................. great.
How are the vegetables?
[4]................. horrible.
How is maths?
It's [5]................. work.
How's English.
It's [6].................!

/ 6

Total / 40

Module 3 Test

Vocabulary

1 Jobs
Look at the pictures. What is the job?

1. .... 2. ....

3. .... 4. ....

☐ / 4

2 Routines
Complete the sentences. Use the words in the box.

brush my teeth	watch TV
get up	go to bed	have lunch

1. I .... at 7 o'clock in the morning.
2. I .... every morning after breakfast.
3. I .... at school at 12 o'clock.
4. In the evening I .... in the living room.
5. At 10 o'clock in the evening, I ....

☐ / 5

Grammar

3 Present Simple
Complete the sentences with a verb in the correct form.

1. They .... breakfast at 7 o'clock.
2. He .... to school by bus.
3. My sister .... TV every day.
4. You .... your teeth.
5. My father .... the washing-up.
6. He .... computer games every day.

☐ / 6

4 at, in, on
Complete the sentences with at, in or on.

1. I go to school .... Monday.
2. He gets up .... quarter past eight.
3. I watch TV .... the morning.
4. I play tennis .... Saturday afternoon.
5. My father goes to work .... 3 o'clock .... the afternoon .... Fridays.
6. I don't do any homework .... the weekend.

☐ / 6

5 Present Simple negative
Make these sentences negative.

1. He's got a car.

....

2. I get up at 7 o'clock.

....

3. I go to school on Saturday.

....

4. My friend does her homework.

....

☐ / 4

6 Present Simple questions
Make questions for these answers.

1. ....?
   I get up at 6 o'clock.
2. ....?
   On Saturdays, I play tennis.
3. ....?
   No, I don't play the guitar.
4. ....?
   Yes, my brother likes football.

☐ / 4

Sentence Builder

7 Put the words in the correct order.

1. play football every I week

....

2. our do every homework We day

....

3. shopping go every They weekend

....

4. month tennis play I every

....

5. at get 8 up o'clock I

....

6. P.E. do Fridays On we

....

☐ / 6

Key Expressions

8 Complete the sentences. Add a verb with ing.

1. I don't like .... homework.
2. I love .... football.
3. I hate .... to the dentist.
4. I like .... books.
5. I don't mind .... television.

☐ / 5

Total ☐ / 40

Module 4 Test

Vocabulary

1 Use one word from each box to complete each sentence.

find	get	look		in	at	to
sit	talk	put		down	out	on

1. Can you .... what time the concert starts?

2. Please .... and be quiet. This is an exam!

3. Come on. .... your boots .... and play football.

4. Do you want to .... my holiday photos?

5. Don't go away! I want to .... you!

6. This is my new car. .... – I can drive you home.

☐ / 6

Grammar

2 Adverbs of frequency
Look at the table and complete the sentences.

All about Lucy
100% listen to music in the evening
80% read magazines
60% do my homework
30% do sport
5% go to the cinema
0% tidy my room

1. She .... listens to music.

2. She .... reads magazines.

3. She .... does her homework.

4. She .... does sport.

5. She .... goes to the cinema.

6. She .... tidies her room.

☐ / 6

3 *There is / are, some / any*
Correct the mistakes. Not all sentences are wrong.

1. There is seventeen students in the class.

....

2. There aren't some books in the room.

....

3. Are there any girls in your family?

....

4. Are there some books on the desk?

....

5. There aren't any posters on the wall.

....

6. There is a teacher in the room.

....

7. There aren't some animals in the park.

....

8. Is there some money in your bag?

....

9. What films is there on TV tonight?

....

10. ..... How many floors are there in this building?

....

☐ / 10

Sentence Builder

4 Put the words in the correct order

1. out friends on go Saturday My often

....

2. never for am school I late

....

3. cinema parents the to My go sometimes

....

4. hardly is She school at ever

....

5. We school games play after computer sometimes

....

6. are garden You the always in

....

7. go usually car to by I school

....

☐ / 7

Key Expressions

5 Complete the sentences. Put one word in each gap.

A: Can you tell me [1].......... to get to your house?

B: Go [2].......... the bank, then [3].......... the road. [4].......... right into Hill Street. There is a cinema [5].......... the corner and, [6].......... the cinema is a bus stop. [7].......... the number five bus from here to the High Street. Get [8].......... the bus and go down the street to the post office. Go [9].......... the post office. My house is [10].......... the left. You can't [11].......... it, it's got a red door.

☐ / 10

Total	/ 40

Module 5 Test

Vocabulary

1 Weather
Complete the gaps.

1. C _ _ _ _ D _
2. _ _ L D
3. _ _ G G _
4. _ O _
5. I _ _ _
6. _ I _ _ Y
7. _ _ R M
8. S _ _ W _

☐ / 8

Grammar

2 Countable and uncountable nouns with *some* and *any*
Complete the sentences with *is / are / isn't / aren't* and *some / any / a*(n).

1. .... there .... animals in the museum?
2. .... there .... pen in your bag?
3. There .... tigers at the South Pole. (✗)
4. There .... water in this cup. (✓)
5. There .... flowers in the garden. (✓)
6. There .... ice at the equator. (✗)
7. There .... cinema on the corner. (✓)
8. .... there .... bus station in your town?

☐ / 8

3 Present Continuous / Present Simple
Complete these sentences using Present Continuous or Present Simple.

1. I .... to school every day.
2. I'm in the car. I'm .... to the cinema.
3. He sometimes .... his homework.
4. Sh, we're .... an exam.
5. Why have you got an umbrella? .... it .... ?
6. .... it rain a lot in Spain?
7. How often .... you .... books?
8. What book .... you .... at the moment?

☐ / 8

Sentence Builder

4 Change the underlined words.
E.g. I've got a dog. ~~The dog's~~ name is Fred.
I've got a dog. It's name is Fred.

1. I've got a car. <u>The car</u> is red.

....

2. John is a student. <u>John</u> is wearing red trousers.

....

3. The animals are cold. <u>The animals</u> are sleeping.

....

4. My mother and I are slim. <u>My mother and I</u> are looking at photos.

....

☐ / 4

5 Put the sentences in the correct order. Match them with the answers a–d.

1. school Why you at aren't?

....

2. your father here isn't Why?

....

3. you nervous Why are

....

4. tennis playing Why aren't you

....

a) Because I have an exam today.
b) Because today is a holiday.
c) Because it's raining.
d) Because he is working.

☐ / 4

Key Expressions

6 Order the dialogue.

1. They're forty pence each. Would you like anything else?
2. Four, please. How much are they?
3. Yes, how many would you like?
4. Good morning, can I help you?
5. That's one pound sixty altogether.
6. No, that's all, thank you.
7. Here you are. Thank you.
8. Good morning. Have you got any cans of cola?

☐ / 8

Total ☐ / 40

Module 6 Test

Vocabulary

1 Transport
Put the letters in the correct order.

1. S U B
2. R T I A N
3. N E L A P
4. R R Y F E
5. P I S H

☐ / 5

Grammar

2 *was* / *were*
Complete the sentences.

1. It .... cold yesterday.
2. I .... scared on the ride. (not)
3. Who .... you with last night?
4. The students .... friendly. (not)
5. I .... at school on Monday.

☐ / 5

3 Past Simple
Put the verbs in brackets into the Past Simple.

Last week I (^{1}go) .... on holiday with my friend. We (^{2}travel) .... by train and (^{3}arrive) .... in Cornwall in the evening. We (^{4}stay) .... in a small hotel. It (^{5}be) .... very nice and very near the sea. On the last day, we (^{6}buy) .... postcards and (^{7}write) .... to our family and friends. We .... (^{8}have) a great time.

☐ / 8

4 Past Simple irregular verbs
Write the past form of each verb.

1. buy ....
2. come ....
3. drink ....
4. learn ....
5. make ....
6. see ....
7. speak ....
8. think ....
9. build ....
10. write ....

☐ / 10

Sentence Builder

5 Rewrite the underlined times with a different time expression.
It is now FRIDAY 18th MAY 2005 at 6p.m.

1. I did my homework on Thursday 17th May at night.
   I did my homework ....

2. I went to the dentist on Thursday 17th May.
   ....

3. My mother started a new job on Friday 11th May 2005.
   ....

4. I went shopping with my friends on Friday 18th May in the morning.
   ....

5. My family went to the mountains on Saturday 12th and Sunday 13th May.
   ....

6. We moved to this town in 2004.
   ....

☐ / 6

Key Expressions

6 Suggestions
Correct the sentences which are wrong.

1. Let's to play football.
   ....

2. Why don't we using the Internet?
   ....

3. We can staying here.
   ....

4. We can to go swimming.
   ....

5. Let's tidying our room.
   ....

6. Let's going to the cinema.
   ....

☐ /6

Total ☐ / 40

Module 7 Test

Vocabulary

1 TV programmes
Match the title with the type of TV programme.

1. *Titanic*   a) documentary
2. *Millionaire*   b) music programme
3. *News at 10*   c) game show
4. *Explorers*   d) film
5. *Top 10 Hits*   e) news   ☐ / 5

2 *ed / ing* adjectives
Choose the correct word in each of the sentences below.

1. That was a really (bored/boring) film.
2. I feel (tired/tiring).
3. Was the holiday (excited/exciting)?
4. The museum was really (interested/interesting).
5. I'm not (interested/interesting) in science.
6. What an (amazed/amazing) book!
7. I always get (bored/boring) in lessons.
8. I like cycling but it's very (tired/tiring).

☐ / 8

Grammar

3 Past Simple negatives
Make these sentences negative.

1. I went to the post office this morning.
....

2. I stayed in a beautiful house.
....

3. My family lived in America.
....

4. We bought a new car.
....

5. I met Robbie Williams last week.
....

6. I thought you were at home.
....

7. I did my homework on the bus.
....

8. We tidied our room.
....

9. I slept on the train.
....

☐ / 9

4 Past Simple questions
Write questions for these answers.

1. ....?
I was born in 1960.

2. ....?
Last year, I lived in Brighton.

3. ....?
I liked history and geography when I was at school.

4. ....?
Yes, I went to the cinema on Friday.

5. ....?
I went to Poland last year.

6. ....?
I travelled by aeroplane.

7. ....?
I went with my family.

8. ....?
Yes, I had a great time!

☐ / 8

Sentence Builder

5 Join the sentences. Use *then* or *after*.
I got up and ¹.............. I had a shower. ².............. my shower, I had breakfast and ³.............. I went to school. ⁴.............. school I played football and ⁵.............. I went home.

☐ /6

Key Expressions

6 Put the words in the correct order to make sentences.

1. are how you? ....
2. you all right are? ....
3. you are okay sure you're? ....
4. a got headache I've ....
5. feel thank all right, I you ....

☐ / 5

Total ☐ / 40

Module 8 Test

Vocabulary

1 Adjectives
Put the letters in the correct order, then match the adjectives with the animals.

1. S O I N O P U O S   **a)** Sloth
   ....
2. L A L T   **b)** Komodo Dragon
   ....
3. Z Y A L   **c)** Blue Whale
   ....
4. O U G R A D N E S   **d)** Snake
   ....
5. N G I T L I N E T L E   **e)** Giraffe
   ....

/ 5

2 Animals
What are the animals?

1. ....   2. ....

3. ....   4. ....

5. ....

/ 5

Grammar

3 Comparatives
Look at the information about Minnie and Shirley. Write comparative sentences.

		Minnie	Shirley
1.	Age	15	17
2.	Height:	1m 56	1m 46
3.	Weight:	54kg	53kg
4.	Intelligence:	****	***
5.	Happiness:	**	****
6.	How relaxed?	*	****
7.	Laziness	**	*
8.	Friendliness	**	****

1. Shirley is .... Minnie.
2. Minnie is .... Shirley.
3. Minnie is .... Shirley.
4. Minnie is .... Shirley.
5. Shirley is .... Minnie.
6. Shirley is .... Minnie.
7. Minnie is .... Shirley.
8. Shirley is .... Minnie.

/8

4 Superlatives and comparatives
Complete the sentences using the correct form of the verb.

1. He is the (tall) .... student in the class.
2. They are the (intelligent) .... people I know.
3. He is (happy) .... than me.
4. Our house is the (small) .... in the street.
5. My mother is (slim) .... than my father.
6. London is (wet) .... than Madrid.
7. Snakes are (dangerous) .... than dolphins.
8. My dog is the (good) .... dog in the world.

/ 8

Sentence Builder

5 Join the sentences using *with*.

1. My brother is tall. He has got blue eyes.
2. Our friends have got a dog. It has got big teeth.
3. Our house is very big. It has got a red door.
4. Our fish is orange. It has got black stripes.
5. Paris is a big city. It has got many beautiful buildings.
6. A giraffe is a tall animal. It has a long neck.

/ 6

Key Expressions

6 Complete the sentences. Use the words in the box.

here	sorry	second	can't
please	just	Can	problem

[1]............... I use your pen, [2]...............?
No, I'm [3]..............., you [4]................
Can you help me with my bags?
Sure, no [5]................
Can I have some more cake?
Sure, [6]............... you are.
Can you do the washing up?
OK, [7]............... a [8]................

/ 8

Total / 40

Module 9 Test

Vocabulary

1 Make jobs from these words.

1. drum
2. sing
3. play
4. teach
5. write
6. swim
7. produce
8. run
9. football
10. work

☐ / 10

Grammar

2 can / can't must / mustn't
There is a mistake in all of these sentences. Correct them.

1. We can't to do homework in class.

....

2. He must to stay at home.

....

3. We can going swimming on Saturday.

....

4. You mustn't eating in class.

....

5. We are can go home at 3 o'clock.

....

6. They must doing the washing up.

....

7. We no must be late for class.

....

8. You mustn't not drive at 150kph.

....

☐ / 8

3 Adverbs / adjectives
Choose the correct word.

1. The concert was (good / well) but the guitarist didn't play very (good / well).

2. The woman in front of us drove very (slow / slowly) but my father usually drives very (fast / fastly).

3. We won the match (easy / easily). The competition was very (easy / easily).

4. Could you speak more (slow / slowly) please? My English isn't very (good / well).

5. He's a (perfect / perfectly) teacher. He always explains things (perfect / perfectly).

6. She's a very (careful / carefully) student. She always writes everything in her book very (careful / carefully).

☐ / 12

Sentence Builder

4 Adverbs / adjectives
Put the sentences into the correct order.

1. fast a got I've car

....

2. fast drives car his He very

....

3. are They students bad really

....

4. a singer She's good

....

5. can very I well sing

....

6. easy is test very a This

....

☐ / 6

Key Expressions

5 Complete the words

1. I passed my exam! W _ _ _ _   _ _ _ _ _ !

2. B _ _   _ _ _ _ _ _ _ _ _ ! You're going too fast!

3. We won the match!

   C _ _ _ _ _ _ _ _ _ _ _ _ _ _ _ _ !

4. W _ _ _ _ _   _ _ _ _ ! There's a car coming!

☐ / 4

Total	/ 40

Module 10 Test

Vocabulary

1 Holidays
Match the words.

A	B
1. go	**a)** at home
2. stay in	**b)** camping
3. go with	**c)** adventure
4. go to the	**d)** friends
5. go on an	**e)** a hotel
6. stay	**f)** beach

/ 6

Grammar

2 *going to* Part i)
Answer these questions with full sentences.

1. Where are you going to go this summer? (Greece)

....

2. What are you going to do at the weekend? (watch TV)

....

3. Are you going to get a job in the summer? (Yes – in a café)

....

Part ii)
Make questions for these answers.

4. I'm going to wear my red dress to the party.

....

5. I'm going to buy him a watch for his birthday.

....

6. I'm going to study history at university.

....

Part iii)
Make these sentences negative.

7. I'm going to write a letter.

....

8. He's going to drive to France.

....

9. We're going to make a cake.

....

/ 9

3 Possessive pronouns
Choose the correct words.

There are two books on the desk. One is (¹my/mine) and one is (²your/yours).
This book has got (³my/mine) name in it.
(⁴Who/Whose) coat is this? Is it (⁵your/yours)?

No, (⁶my/mine) is blue. I think it's (⁷her/hers).
We're going on holiday together. (⁸Who/Whose) car are we going to drive?
I think we're going to go in (⁹our/ours), it's bigger than (¹⁰your/yours).

/ 10

Sentence Builder

4 Future time expressions
Change the underlined words for time expressions.

1. We're going to France <u>today in the night</u>.

....

2. They're going to come to our house <u>the day after today</u>.

....

3. We're going to go to our grandparents' house <u>next Saturday and Sunday</u>.

....

4. He's going to buy a house <u>the week after this</u>.

....

5. We're going to go to Disneyland <u>this year in the summer</u>.

....

6. They're not going to come to see us <u>the year after this year in the summer</u>.

....

/ 6

Key Expressions

5 Complete the sentences. Use the words in the box.

Do want Would like to sorry can't I'd love

¹.............. you like to come to my party tonight?
Yes, ².............. love to!
Do you ³.............. to go swimming on Thursday?
No, I'm ⁴.............. , I can't.
Would you ⁵.............. to go to the cinema next week?
Yes, I'd ⁶.............. to.
⁷.............. you want ⁸.............. watch this DVD tonight?
I ⁹.............. tonight. I'm going out with my parents.

/ 9

Total / 40